Campaigning to Win

Campaigning to Win

Gary O. Bosley

To order additional copies of this book, contact:
Xlibris Corporation
1-888-7-XLIBRIS
www.Xlibris.com
Orders@Xlibris.com

Contents

12   177

Information

13   187

The Candidate

14   203

Citizens Groups

15   208

A Final Word: Tying It All Together

16   213

References and Notes

Introduction to the Manual

I. What do we know?

On election day, the winner has received at least fifty percent of the vote plus one. Votes determined the winner. Winners were not determined by the number of newsreleases issued, number of mailings, party registration, name identification percentages, nor size of the research committee on the campaign, etc.

The method for winning presented in this work is based upon the simplest of structures, the simplest of approaches, and the most straightforward way to win:

asking for the vote.

This is accomplished through a three pronged front, which focuses on campaigning, not the campaign. Once this approach is understood and acted upon, the three prongs or parts of campaigning will move forward mutually reinforcing each other. The three prongs are: 1. The campaign for money. 2. The campaign for getting the support of the influence centers in the community likely to be on your side. 3. The campaign for the mass vote.

Each of these three areas must be campaigned in. The need for money is obvious. The need for the mass vote appeal is obvious. But, the tie-in between the two through the good offices of influential people in the district in not obvious. The simple and direct method of seeking out influential support as outlined in this work is what gives it a unique emphasis. This is covered in the chapter on the **district inventory**.

The classic three resource variables of campaigns have come to be considered almost in the light of a cliché, but they take on added meaning, when considering the likely status of a campaign versus its opponents'. The three variables are, of course, **time, money,** and **manpower.**

A challenger in all too many cases knows he or she will be outspent by the incumbent. Manpower, as a resource variable, is very "costly" in terms of "efforts expended versus benefits gained." *The* variable, then, which must be focused upon for there to be any realistic chance for success is **tim**e. Again, the simplicity and straightforward approach of *Campaigning to Win* fills this bill.

II. How Do We Know?

We know it because we've either done it, watched it, or found examples of it. We know the above by recognizing it in so much of the literature for campaigns and campaigning. This is why we have given so many references by way of documentation. The writer has managed campaigns, consulted on campaigns, and been a sacrificial lamb candidate himself.

This work comes about as a result of the writer having seen so many candidates, campaign steering committees, and workers, get lost in the minutia of "technique." If the candidates had had the right focus in the first place, they could have concentrated upon moving forward and actually getting things done. The hollow ring of "We are going to . . ." tolls throughout losing campaigns, which never made the transition to "We have done . . ."

By way of showing how we know, we first start off this manual of direct action by highlighting what campaigns and candidates **don't** know. The first part of the manual concentrates upon the problem of "issues." The basic problem is what issues **are not.** We also cover the problem of "issue education," otherwise known as "voter education."

After disposing of what campaigns don't know, we proceed into the areas of campaign organization and vote targeting. Then, we concentrate upon three "fronts," which are the action thrusts for winning, as in war.

We cover the traditional aspects of campaigning such as newsrelease use, issues research, candidate speech making, literature, media, and precinct organization, etc. But, it is done in the context of the implicit definition of campaigning given above: *campaigning is asking for votes*.

III. So What?

Small campaigns (any campaign without a large full time, paid staff) must start out focused and expend resources wisely. This work gives a stripped down, lean version of what must be done to win. A campaign can do more, or accomplish the goals outlined here with a bigger bang, and win. However, a campaign will ignore the goals and needs demonstrated here at its peril.

Political Misinformation

A losing conservative Republican candidate for Congress told a local newspaper, just after the election, that he was "still convinced the district is far more conservative" than the winning incumbent congressman. The paper quoted him: "The people just don't know [the congressman] is out of step with them." [1] The loser had further comments about the ability of the people "to look at the issues and make an intelligent judgment."

There followed in the newspaper, four days later, a rejoinder to the loser's comments, in the "letters to the editor section." The incumbent congressman's forces had made effective use of the "letters to the editor" section during the campaign and they got in one last lick. The writer chided the loser for not taking the loss graciously. The letter finished by saying: "Again, I think it very small of a man of [the candidate's] standing to belittle the average voter just because he did not get elected. I am glad to see the time when a man can be elected by the 'average voter' instead of a select few." [2]

Over the years, observers of the nation's political scene have watched as elected politicians throughout the country continued to be liberal, while most polls were indicating that the mood of "the people" was progressively more and more conservative. To the great consternation of conservatives, the voter's "mood" did not seem to translate into votes, until 1994.

The editorial pages of newspapers and magazines over the years have presented untold numbers of columnists grasping and grappling to answer the apparent paradox of voter mood and why it was not translated into votes. Since the problem has been countrywide, and since "macropolitical" (i.e., broad brush, "Watergate did it") explanations do not give adequate reasons over time, an analogy from economics may give some guidance.

Murray Rothbard in his book, *America's Great Depression*, stated: "The main problem that a theory of depression must explain is: *why is there a sudden general cluster of business errors?* (emphasis his) . . . Business activity moves along nicely with most business firms making handsome profits. Suddenly, without warning, conditions change and the bulk of business firms are experiencing losses . . . In short, how did all the country's astute businessmen come to make such errors together. . . ?"[3]

Rothbard answered the question that he posed with a disarmingly simple answer. The essence of his answer was that an aberration with money, which is a part of every financial transaction, was the main cause.

Using such an intellectual spotlight politically, Rothbard's answer could be translated into political terms for political purposes here, viz.: "If voters are conservative (or anti-incumbent), why do challengers (or conservative candidates) do so consistently poorly?" Certainly, liberals or incumbents do not have a corner on political craftsmanship. Nor, do they have all the money.

The answer to the challenger's (or conservative's) dilemma could likewise be something that is a part of every political "transaction" or what would be considered to be "political currency." This is nothing more than what all campaigns deal in: information (issues).

The answer just may be in "issues" and the way candidates and campaigns *perceive* the use of issues.

Ask a conservative who is in a campaign against a liberal if the conservative has any winning issues. Virtually all such conservatives will say that the question is ludicrous, that if anything, there were too many issues and that all would be "winners" against the opposition.

However, consider what Peter Wychoff, an expert on investment psychology, has to say about opinions: "unanimity of opinion is a dangerous thing; and one way to win . . . is to avoid what most others are doing." [4] This is, of course, contrary opinion. Harry Schultz, author of Financial Tactics and Terms for the Sophisticated International Investor, defines contrary opinion as: "A . . . theory based on the concept that the 'mass man' is generally wrong." [5]

Since issues are the common denominator of all challengers and conservatives, it is the thesis of this work that these campaigns are using issues in the wrong way. This is because **their perceptions of what issues in fact are, are wrong**. This misperception comes from the national media (not from any sort of conspiracy, however). Furthermore, the error of the media is compounded by incumbent politicians. Based upon these errors, *political activism becomes confused with "voter education."* Examples of problems are legion. They can even be traced in some sincere but misguided attempts on the part of some individuals to bring about political action.

Political activists consider themselves to be well informed. They usually take pride in being informed. Yet, quite often, a gathering of activists would find them to be far apart in their thinking as to what the *most* important issue at any given time might be. Also, if they were to arrive at an agreement on a particular issue, they would then disagree as to what facet of that issue was the most important. Consider the problem of how to attack "inflation" as an issue.

While there could be many different sources of information that activists were using, there would nevertheless be an undercurrent of similarity of information flow. That is, that while they may not all be referring to the latest issue of *Time* magazine, nevertheless, there would be rough agreement as to what the "current" issues were. This continuity is in fact based upon what the current media is covering. *Time*, *Newsweek*, and *U.S. News & World Report*, and others, exert major control over what is being discussed by way of "issues," along with national TV and newspapers.

No less a person than David Rockefeller, at the time chairman of the board of Chase Manhattan bank, made the following observation along the lines of the media determining issues. In an article he wrote on the problems encountered by business in working with "ideas," he stated: "One consultant on government relations says he measures the importance of public issues with a ruler. He takes major newspapers and magazines and adds up the column inches devoted to each public issue." [6]

Newsmagazines and other media are being paid by their audience to present news. The same holds for election coverage as news. The media analyzes election races before the election, and then analyzes the results after the election. Political activists (as potential challengers for an elected position) or, those on the conservative side, are usually activists due to their interests and inclinations toward political matters. As such, these interests have led them to imbibe the media's political information coverage over a considerable period of time.

Except for egregious cases, rarely, if ever, does someone ask if the media might not be wrong in its coverage. [This is not to confuse the question of obvious media bias with that of the problem of coverage. (Edith Efron in her book, *The News Twisters*, has documented bias quite well.)] Consider the following. If the media were wrong as to what, and how, issues were important, then the people who have developed their attitudes from exposure to the media would be wrong also!

Therefore, where does the media pay the closest attention? Top of the ballot races get the most media attention for obvious reasons: more people are interested. Presidential races get coverage in many cases to ridiculous extremes, often obscuring what is in fact really important. Gubernatorial and senatorial races get fair national coverage, usually to the degree that something "different" is available to the media: a prominent name, a theme of national attention, or extremes of effort. Lower level election races get considerably less exposure.

Issues

The common denominator of election coverage is the handling of "issues." Issues are something that are for candidates, against candidates, above the surface, below the surface, or anywhere else! Issues are reported as philosophical or ad hominum (against the "person" of the candidate). The tired cliché of a candidate who announces his/her candidacy and states that he/she will run "on the issues" seems to be on the mind of most political reporters.

The plethora of words used in election reportage tends to result in a caricature of the process. The October 21, 1974 issue of *Time* stated on page 27 that: "It sometimes seems as if the archetypal candidate of campaign '74 is one who stages a 750-mile walking tour across the state, rejects all contributions above $100, rarely lets on whether he is a Democrat or a Republican and approaches everything with deadly earnestness." This was a good summation of the image that candidates presented at that time. However, it was an image and it was presented to the media. The media "bought" it and passed it on to the public that was watching.

Consider the easy acceptance by the media as to what constitutes an issue. In 1968 the *National Observer* published a book on the approaching elections. The book was called *Newsbook*. In the section which covered Richard Nixon's efforts, much was made of Nixon's experience in foreign affairs. According to the book, Nixon " . . . hopes to ride this knowledge right in to the White House." The reader [in the view of the author of the story in *Newsbook*, we are led to believe] immediately had visions of voters entering the voting booth with newsclip images in mind from the "Six o'clock News" of Nixon stepping off a plane in a foreign country, ready to save America's interests. The country would be safe with a man of Nixon's foreign affairs experience sitting in the White House . . .

Consider the following example of a journalist's idea of a "solid issue," which presumably would propel voters into the voting booth for a candidate. In 1974 the Republican nominee for governor in California was Houston Flournoy. *Time* magazine informed its readers in its issue of October 21, 1974, that: "Flournoy also has a solid issue to work with: Reagan is leaving California with a surplus of about $300 million after inheriting a deficit of $350 million dollars . . ." Jerry Brown won the election against Flournoy.

U.S. News & World Report had it all figured out for the elections of 1970. The October 5, 1970, issue stated that, "The central issue in congressional races is the record of the Nixon Administration—with most Republicans supporting the president, and many Democrats attacking the Administration's management of the national economy." This was newsworthy??? It said that Republicans were partial to a Republican president and the Democrats weren't!!!

With pre-election coverage somewhat cloudy, one wonders if the media does much better on giving insights into the results of election contests. *Time* covered John Danforth's U.S. Senate victory in Missouri on page 44 in the November 15, 1976 issue. It said, "Danforth can be a tough political infighter on issues he cares about—notably, the curse of Big Government."

Equally less than penetrating was the *Time* coverage on November 20, 1972, on page 38 which explained how James Abnor in South Dakota beat Patrick McKeever, a six year staffer for George McGovern. "Abnor managed to parlay the voters mistrust of the McKeever-McGovern platform into a narrow victory."

A reader interested in election cause and effect would have found little succor in the quest for knowledge in yet another *Time* analysis. The magazine reported in complete seriousness on the Democratic primary victory of Mary Rose Oakar, Cleveland City councilwoman, who had no Republican opposition in November. It stated in the November 15, 1976 issue on page 48: "Oakar won her decisive Democratic primary nomination by pointing out that among several major candidates, she was the only non-lawyer and the only woman."

The foregoing are not isolated examples of election coverage. They represent a "mainstream" journalistic offering to the public. A reader consistently given such pap almost necessarily absorbs "impressions" which form vague images of how politicians get elected.

From time to time, the media gets close to "real" coverage. However, the form and the result are not enlightening. *Time* on November 15, 1968 came close. It said, "Republican Manual Lujan Jr. Upset five-term Democratic Representative Thomas G. Morris mainly on the basis of local economic issues." In the same issue, *Time* focused on incumbents who won their election race. However, it said: "Even in those districts where seats did change party hands, the results seemed to depend far more on individual personalities and local conditions than on broad national issues—Viet Nam, law and order, inflation . . ." Two years later, *U.S. News & World Report* had something similar to say. In the issue of October 19, 1970, it stated: "In state elections, the outcome may hinge more on local conditions of personalities than on national issues or the popularity of the president."

Politicians Add to Problem

If the election coverage of candidates by the media is less than penetrating on the part of the reporters, statements made by politicians regarding what is really important only reinforce the media and its view. This is because the same reporters select the quotations of the politicians who were originally carried in the news. On September 23, 1974, *Time* quoted the G.O.P. state chairman in Colorado commenting on the 1974 senate race between Gary Hart and incumbent Peter Dominick. Said Dwight Hamilton regarding Gary Hart, "He's an old pol, a soul brother of McGovern.

He's going to have to answer every one of the issues McGovern stood for in 1972." Hart won the race.

U.S. News & World Report quoted House Republican leader John J. Rhodes concerning the 1978 congressional elections in the January 2, 1978, issue: " . . . Rhodes says that Carter will be 'the issue' in the 1978 campaign."

After all the words and heat generated by the media in its efforts to cover "the issues" and report what made for winning elections, remarkably little light seems to have shined. But, if the media has this problem, the 1970 congressional elections showed that politicians had it also. *U.S. News & World Report* headlined on October 26, 1970, "'70 Campaign Takes a New Turn." The article hit what it considered to be the "enigma" of the campaign, that President Nixon was throwing the prestige of the presidency into a drive to elect Republicans to Congress.

If anyone would have known what the "issues" were at that time, the president, Nixon himself, certainly should have. *U.S. News & World Report* quoted a presidential advisor as saying, "Richard Nixon is calling the shots himself. He knows exactly what the political situation is in the country." Nixon made campaign appearances for 17 candidates for governor, 11 lost. He made appearances for 21 senatorial candidates, 13 lost. Nixon made appearances for 236 candidates for the House of Representatives, 122 lost.

The results of the Nixon campaign blitz were not all negative, however. According to the same tally by *U.S. News & World Report*, the Republicans lost fewer House seats than average for the political party in power during an off year election. It reported that the average loss since 1950 had been 29 seats to that time. The Republicans lost only 9 seats.

Incumbency

The whole idea of "issues" as reported by the media, or even suggested by politicians in power, appears to pale in importance when considered in light of "incumbency." News magazines use page after page reporting on political races. Politicians expend reams of paper issuing "news releases." Yet, after each election, invariably, reports show that the vast majority of incumbents won re-election. The election recapitulation by *Time* in 1968 head-lined: "The House: The Year of the Incumbent." In 1970 only 12 incumbents were defeated for re-election to the House of Representatives. The *Time* article for 1972 on House races was headlined: "The House: Vintage Year for the Incumbent."

While 1974 was supposed to have changed some political "rules" due to the Watergate mess, 1976 showed that the old rules were just as strong as ever. The freshman Democrats of the "Watergate class," who had won in 1974, by and large won re-election in what had been safe Republican districts.

In planning for the 1978 congressional races, the national G.O.P. was reported to be not even considering serious conten-tion for many of what had been, up to 1974, safe Republican seats. Their efforts were going to be focused on districts that were open due to retirements. "At least we start even in the open seat races," said Steven Stockmeyer, executive director of the Na-tional Republican Congressional Committee, at that time."[7]

The advantages of incumbency are likewise enjoyed in state representative races, county contests, and city elections. Being an incumbent seems to transcend anything as ephemeral as "is-sues."

It would appear that a political aspirant might almost have to resign himself to waiting for a seat to come open by virtue of the incumbent leaving the scene for whatever reason. If incumbency is the magic ingredient for political success, it would appear fool-ish to challenge an incumbent. However, political reality does not support the view of putting one's organizing manuals on ice until a seat becomes open.

The LBJ landslide of 1964 was accompanied by an increase of 37 in Democratic held House seats. Clearly, many Republi-can incumbents were beaten. Yet, then, in 1966, there were more

Republicans added to the House rolls than the Democrats had ousted in 1964. The year 1966 was not the year for Democrat incumbents.

Incumbency and the capriciousness of a political cycle for incumbents certainly would make for dry reporting on the part of the media. Undaunted, however, the media presses forward with its analyses of issues, candidates, and miscellaneous appurtenances in election races.

It is not the intention, here, to indict the media for inaccuracy, mis-reporting, or distortion. Quite simply, the media is giving the public what both sides perceive to be in demand. Overviews and interesting tidbits make for interesting news. The majority of readers are not interested in how many precincts were organized, how many "dear friend" cards were mailed, etc. Furthermore, the media does not have the time or resources to probe into very many races. Nor does the popular media have the expertise to pass on what is "really" happening in election contests. However, the point to understand is that people who are interested in visceral cause and effect in election contests do absorb impressions from the popular media. This is even as the mass media has turned away from more substantial reportage of election contests.

It becomes apparent, from the above offerings of popular media analyses of various election races, that the "insights" are more gossamer than penetrating. A reader, hungry for substance, would have to turn to other sources for sustenance, away from the popular media.

Other Media

Moving away from *Time* and to the *California Journal* is additionally instructive. The *California Journal* bills itself as "the monthly analysis of state government and politics." It is highly regarded and considered authoritative in many circles, even with its somewhat liberal tilt. In the October 1976 issue, the *California Journal* carried an analysis of the state assembly race in the 75th Assembly district. In California, state assembly districts are roughly one half the size of a congressional seat in terms of population represented.

The article was titled "Duel in the Sun" and authored by James Brooks, editorial page editor of the *Palm Springs Desert Sun*. The contest was billed as "one of the most hotly contested legislative races." The seat at stake had been considered solid Republican until 1974, when the incumbent was beaten by a slim margin, 40,561 to 39,132. Going into the 1976 race, the Republicans felt they could beat Democrat Tom Suitt who had won by such a thin margin two years earlier.

The article called the forty year old Suitt a "full time political person." His Republican opponent was Riverside County Supervisor, Al McCandless, 49. McCandless had sold his GMC auto dealership to devote full time to the political battle. Both candidates won their primaries by very convincing margins. The political registration was 48 percent Democrat to 45 percent Republican. Clearly, the race appeared to be a classic set piece battle between the two parties.

The article by Brooks indicated that there were no extraneous issues or scandals publicly perceived. The leadership of both parties was pouring manpower and money into the race. The article ended on the following note: "Except for those who have been out in the summer sun too long, the all important 75th Assembly district race remains too close to call."

The results? Suitt won by a landslide, 62,735 to 47,372, or 57% to 43%. This was at the same time that California was carried by President Ford by a slim margin. Republican S.I. Hayakawa beat incumbent U.S. Senator John Tunney in that election, also. However, what is worse from a political analyst's view, the two House seats which divided most of the 75th Assembly District were won by incumbent Republicans. The Republican hangover after the election had to be more than aspirin could handle. Yet, after having seen what the political pundits had to say by way of analysis of the contest before the election, their failure was just as great as the Republican's.

More Fallacies

That there is a great misunderstanding on the part of the media and even politicians regarding election "cause and effect" soon becomes apparent.

Most campaigns at the congressional level and below have steering committees of "kitchen cabinets," which consist of well meaning friends, acquaintances and perhaps some "professionals" connected with the candidate. It is the collective judgment of these people, which focuses the campaign, or un-focuses it, as the case may be. These political activists are the ones who have absorbed much of what the media serves up as political news. However, there remains further potential for misunderstanding. Not only have political activists absorbed "news" about election races, but they also have absorbed the tremendous blurring of what are considered political matters with what are considered campaign matters.

Consider the various obituaries and analyses of the obituaries of the Republican Party. Because the Republicans had done so poorly for so many years, every political scientist and political activist could cite reasons for the party's' decline. Much appeared in the media on the problem: (The same media that misses on analyzing "issues" and elections.)

Fortune magazine carried an incredible article in its September 1977 issue titled, "The Unmaking of the Republican Party." The article was incredible because of the supposed weight of authority of the political scientist who authored it. Everett Carl Ladd Jr. wrote the article and was identified as a political scientist at the University of Connecticut at Storrs and director of its Social Science Data Center.

Professor Ladd gave his readers "amazing" insights in the article. He said on page 102: "Republicans of all persuasions agree that their party has too negative an image, that it should set forth its own positive ideas more attractively, and that it should make a more effective connection between the feelings in its gut and the aspirations of the American people." He continued, " . . . coherent and energizing public philosophies—those which are progressive" in the sense that they are able to move the country in a direction desired by much of the population—don't exactly grow on trees." Later he said, "the alienation of informed opinion and the intellectual community from the G.O.P. means that the party lacks the sort of people whose contributions are crucial to the formulation of an alternative to the liberal orthodoxy."

Any college freshman in "Poli-Sci 1" would have received an "F" for writing an essay, which spoke of "gut feelings" in the context of a national political party. And, while the substance of the professor's article in *Fortune* was essentially worthless, he provided a service for the purposes of this work. He demonstrated in public his ignorance of the difference between matters of political philosophy as compared to what would be considered to be approaches to election contests. This is the same ignorance exhibited by part time political activists and many full time ones.

Even Republican National Chairman (at that time) Bill Brock, who managed to lose his U.S. Senate seat in Tennessee as an incumbent, still considered himself an authority on electoral matters. In addition, he showed the world his ignorance of the difference between electoral philosophy and electoral mechanics. Norman Miller, the *Wall Street Journal* Washington bureau chief, quoted Brock's thinking about the Republican party. "We ignore, do not relate and are irrelevant to the average American . . . Too many voters see us not as a party, but as a narrow, vested interest, a barely disguised front for big corporations, bankers and the chamber of commerce."[8] Miller's article was titled, "Ailing G.O.P. May Not Recover." Toward the end of the article, he had an interesting observation: " . . . it is alarming to some Republicans that Jimmy Carter is bidding to steal traditional

Republican issues with his talk of balancing the budget, cutting red tape and making the bureaucracy efficient. If he succeeds, or makes discernible progress toward these goals, the Republicans could be co-opted." Mr. Miller does not state what the likely results would be of Carter co-opting here-to-fore *losing* Republican "issues." Other examples of results from the misunderstanding and commingling of "issues," "electoral mechanics," and "political philosophy" are readily available. Erroneous diagnoses lead to bad prescriptions.

Education Versus Activism

As liberal programs poured forth from the liberal Congresses of the 1960's and 1970's, well meaning individuals, businesspeople, and politicians exhorted their fellow citizens to "educate" the public as to the deleterious consequences of many of the liberal's fond programs. Therefore, in the sense of educating the public to become concerned, the programs were good. However, in the sense that political activists misconstrued "education" in the sense of "political activism," then the education efforts were not at all on target.

Senator Barry Goldwater addressed the American Iron and Steel Institute in Washington D.C. in February 1974. The title of this talk was "Business Must Educate Public."[9] Goldwater described the many problems facing business. The problems were becoming worse as "liberal" legislation worked more and more hardships on business. His prescription for business had three areas of action that business should take. The first one was to organize "truth teams" to "go into the community rooms of the schools, the union clubs and Rotary clubs—that they appear on local TV and radio to confront the critics and debate the issues." His second suggestion was "to compete effectively in the crucial market place of ideas . . . the *intellectual* (his emphasis) market place—the deepwater mainstream of idea formulation which has the most pervasive impact on public attitudes and public policies." Goldwater's third task for business called for political activism.

Conservative political activists applaud speeches such as Sen. Goldwater gave, but little seems to come from such talks.

In April 1975, Senator James L. Buckley of New York gave an address to the Petroleum Geologists in Dallas, Texas.[10] In a thoroughly intellectual speech, Buckley described many problems the energy industry has having. He also got to the heart of the matter. "Have no doubt about it. The free enterprise philosophy is being attacked, moreover, in the name of a new regulatory ethic, promulgated by antibusiness critics in the academy and in government, and implemented by the ever ravenous bureaucracy in Washington . . ." Later, he stated: "Bills affecting the energy industry have been introduced this year, or are in the last stages of preparation, that are awesome in their sweep. They can only be described as revolutionary in their potential impact on traditional concepts of the appropriate role of government in our business affairs."

Just as Goldwater, Buckley offered three areas in which: "American business leaders must work to stem the tide that is running so rapidly against the concept of free enterprise . . . First of all, they must become more directly concerned over the general level of public appreciation of how that system works. This will require a vast educational effort to remind Americans how their economy works. Secondly, every businessman who cares about the future must somehow involve himself in the political process . . . Finally, representatives of every sector of American business must begin lobbying first and foremost for the preservation of a political environment in which our economy can continue to prosper."

Again, political activists applauded the call to arms. Yet, how much effort do calls for education bring forth? What does "somehow involve himself in the political process" mean? The Goldwater and Buckley statements left too much open ended.

However, it is not only well-meaning politicians who advise education. Businesspeople have been advising the same thing for quite some time.

Lee A. Iacocca, when he was still Vice President of the car and truck group for Ford Motor Company in 1967, addressed the University of California Executive Program. His address was called, "The Responsibility of Business for Promoting Economic Growth." In his concluding remarks, he said: "The development of a healthy blend of freedom and responsibility in our nation's economic affairs depends upon the extent to which the American people understand their stake in the free enterprise system."

Somewhat more recently, Raymond J. Markham, Vice President and Director of Marketing for Encyclopedia Britannica, had a call to action essay widely published, titled, "Myths About Business that Threaten Your Future."[11] The gist of the presentation was that the public perception of corporations was badly distorted. The essay outlined the problem and suggested some action. The beginning of the call to action starts, "Consumers must be made to realize . . ." He continued: "What I am proposing is a national coalition of all business groups, crossing industry lines. Imagine a well conceived, well executed national program designed to educate and "sell" our system—and its unparalleled benefits—to the rest of society. The communication tools are available to us—and we know how to use them intelligently: Paid and public service advertising; public relations that meets the all-important tests of objectivity and credibility; speakers' bureaus; and political action on a grass roots, one-on-one level, to name a few."

A call to action such as the foregoing always warms the heart of a political activist. Yet, that is as far as most such programs get. Unfortunately, such calls to action tend to flood political literature and obscure the basic political action that is really necessary. Each of the above examples sought some political action, implied or explicit. But, the political action was secondary, after the call for education. There-in lies the problem, from the point of view of real political action.

While nothing has usually followed from "education exhortations," there was one time in the U.S. that such a program was put together with gusto. The program was the famous Liberty League of the 1930's.

An excellent exposition of the Liberty League has been done by David A. Pietrusza.[12] "The particular business and objects" of the League, said its articles of incorporation, "shall be to defend and uphold the Constitution of the United States and to gather and disseminate information that (1) will teach the necessity of respect for the rights of persons and property as fundamental to every form of government and (2) will teach the duty of government to encourage and protect individual and group initiative and enterprise, to foster the right to work, earn, save and acquire property . . ." As one of the League's pamphlets observed, " . . . government disregard for property rights soon leads to disregard for other rights. A bureaucracy or despotism that robs citizens of their property does not like to be haunted by its victims."

The League, according to Pietrusza, "was clearly not some fringe organization. It was wealthy and it was respectable—eminently respectable." Stellar names of the industrial world were behind the League and they put very sizable money into the League's activities. The formation of the League was announced in August 1934. It was to be a non-partisan or bipartisan attempt to topple the New Deal by 1936.

The League became a truly national effort at educating the country in conservative political thought. In 1935 it raised as much money as the two major parties combined. A major pamphlet campaign was instituted which distributed millions of pamphlets nationwide. A full time staff of over fifty people worked in conjunction with various state headquarters of the League.

But after truly monumental efforts, 1936 and the debacle of Alf Landon took most the wind out of the League's sales. Public efforts were suspended and it became a research office only, analyzing legislation.

Of course, during the peak period of the League's efforts, the opposition to the League was not quiet. In the battle for listener's hearts, Senator Joseph T. Robinson said: "I think you people read of the accounts of the severe winter through which we have just passed. As the Liberty League implies, think how demoralizing it must have been, with the thermometer ten degrees below zero, to have Uncle Sam supplying funds to repair the damaged shoes of children who were forced to trudge back and forth to school. The Du Pont brothers must have been shocked [by] . . . that classic example of undermining the moral fiber of children on relief."

Surely, the Liberty League qualifies as a positive example in the scale of its efforts as a national educational effort, if not the results. Surely, the founding of a comparable organization at this time would more than fill the various calls to action by the senators and businessmen quoted above. However, just as surely, such a large organization through sheer size and weight, cannot attain a sharp focus.

The call for an educational effort is necessarily predicated upon the idea "if only the people knew." However, that was the plaintive cry of the losing congressional candidate quoted at the beginning of this chapter. The argument has come full circle. "If only the people knew what?" If only the people knew the *issues*. And, there again, the argument comes full circle.

Most political activists tend to fall into this trap. Their idea is to get "the" information to the people. The belief is that people would then vote for the candidate who had "educated them." This constant confusion between issues, education, and political activity for electoral purposes is seen in many disagreements between people discussing "politics"—"politics" oriented to the ballot box.

Perhaps, part of this confusion could be laid to rest by the following. Some years ago, the Joint Council on Economic Education released the results of a survey which showed that more than half of the 20,000 high school students surveyed did not know the difference between collectivism and free enterprise. Also, most did not know that the U.S. economic system was based on free enterprise.[13] Furthermore, only seven per cent of American educators have had any economic training.[14] In the face of such widespread economic ignorance, why should we believe that the degree of political education is greater? Time and time again polls have shown that the majority of people cannot name their state legislators. No one would care to bet against the proposition that more people knew the name of Archie Bunker's wife at the time than knew the name of their Congressman, let alone what the congressman stood for . . .

To emphasize: the thesis offered here is that election efforts should not be confused with educational efforts. Educational efforts are to be encouraged and condoned, but they should not be allowed to dilute election/ballot box efforts, which is unfortunately quite often the case.

"Opinion-leader" types of education, such as that done so effectively by Mobil Oil in much of the leading print media, about the energy crunch years ago, were very good. However, again, such efforts don't elect candidates to office.

Sincere But Misguided

Occasionally, public frustration with the course of national political developments will make for an embarrassing, but also instructive, public display of ignorance. Consider the following example. Individuals prone to do the following are sincere in their efforts, but are only to be pitied for their lack of understanding of their own political system.

On Tuesday, July 23, 1968, there appeared a full-page advertisement in the *Oakland*, California, *Tribune*. The ad was headlined, "My Open Letter to You—the People." It started: "This is the time in my life when the anger of being misled is causing me to become directly involved in the future of my nation. I am thirty-nine years old, a father of six fine children, the president of a small corporation, homeowner, citizen, veteran and taxpayer. I have worked hard at being self-sufficient and self-reliant. I have also spent a good number of years assuming that our country was being well led and administered . . . The past year has led me to the full realization of what our destiny as a nation will be if we continue with our present form of governmental policies. It is unbelievable that such a great many people can be so mislead."

The ad was about 2,500 words long. It had, as major headings: politics, people, students, Vietnam, foreign policy, civil rights, law and order, and gun control. Under the last heading of "issues," the writer said, "I really believe there are reasonable solutions to our problems . . . If we are to save this great country called America, then we need to work together for a common goal, learning to live together, finding beneficial solutions to our problems and in peace."

The writer finished his message saying that he was sick of politics, that he was neither Republican nor Democrat. He said: "I want first-class honest citizens with one desire—the good of the people, to lead my nation. I am this type of man. If what I propose is the type of direction you want for our nation, then I need your support. Together and united we can accomplish these goals—divided we shall continue to fail." It was signed, Paul K. Davis, American. It also carried a coupon that stated: "Dear Mr. Davis: Please carry on with your program. You have my support. (Or) Please do not carry on with your program."

In an article about the ad in the same edition, the *Tribune* stated that Davis was not sure "what happens next." "I'm not a politician," he emphasized. "Before I get out on a limb, I'd like to find out if others feel as I do. If I get a strong response, I will meet with the people who are interested to see what we can do. If the response is not good, I'll forget it." The irony of the matter was that he continued to reiterate that he was not politically inclined, but that he understood that any action would probably have to take place on the political level. "It might involve supporting one of the candidates now in the field . . . It might mean the formation of a new party." The *Tribune* opined, "If the response here is good he would hope to spread statewide, and finally across the country."

The next day, the paper reported that Davis had received more than 200 letters and about 50 phone calls. That was as far as it went. Ten years later, Mr. Davis, through his secretary, told this writer in a telephone conversation, that the whole exercise had been a waste of time, effort, and money.

Davis' "brothers in frustration" have continued (over time) with similar exercises, however. *The Wall Street Journal* for February 24, 1978, carried a full page advertisement which head-lined, "Sleep Not My Country." In a rambling polemic, readers were offered sterotypical lines. "As I travel from coast to coast and border to border and talk with people from all walks of life, I have never seen such frustration and pessimism . . . How did we get into the deplorable condition we are in today?" The author gave some obscure advise supposedly to Jimmy Carter, but it was unclear. The author then identified himself as Alton S. Newell, Chairman, Newell Manufacturing Company

Then on March 1, 1978, another full page ad ran in *The Wall Street Journal*, this time by Dresser Industries. It urged America's 25 million shareholders to "become involved." This ad finished its message politely and suppliantly: "Dresser believes that Congress and the Administration should review existing governmental policies and programs and carefully evaluate new proposals with the objective of achieving a proper balance between the benefits and the costs of current and future governmental activity."

The degree of political naiveté exhibited by these public pronouncements was shocking. Unfortunately, such is more often the rule than the exception. However, in keeping with the focus of *Campaigning*, the point here is not to indict businesspeople for political naivete.

The point is to avoid well intentioned, but naive, people having any sort of deleterious effects in a political campaign. Because a campaign is comprised of a small number of people, its course can be affected by the ignorance of one person.

Consider what happened to a professional political consult-ant who tried to change some naivete. Alan J. Otten, in *The Wall Street Journal,* did an article on some experiences encountered by David Keene in an attempt to heighten the political impact of some business political action committees. "This past winter, Mr. Keene decided it might be a good idea, particularly after last fall's election results, if someone who really knew politics set out to advise these corporate PAC's on just how to work most effec-tively for probusiness candidates and probusiness causes. He put the idea to several dozen leading corporations—and there wasn't a taker in the bunch." Said, Keene: "All of them insisted that there wasn't any need of special expertise to undertake politi-cal action. After all, they told me, everyone knows politics."

Others have commented on the same phenomenon. Theodore White pointed out, "There is no businessman who, when intro-duced as financial chairman to a campaign, does not become overnight an expert on television, images and voter impulses.[15]

2

Campaigns

A campaign, any campaign, is simply a set of actions by a group of people in pursuit of a specific objective.

Service Club Elections

In a service club election, it is understood that a majority of votes is needed to win. If there are 100 people in the club casting ballots, 51 votes wins. The problem, then, is to find those 51 votes. The problem is not finding 51 enemies to the opposition, although that would win the number needed. That is too divisive and negative and would probably fall of its own weight. The basic procedure would be to identify the various cliques and groupings in the club, which would be favorable to the particular candidacy of a particular person/candidate.

Contact would be made with the individuals and groups and votes would be solicited. At the point where all favorably disposed votes had been contacted, and especially, if the 51 votes could not be found, it would become necessary to work harder. That work would probably take the form of wooing other voters by finding out what their interests were and attempting to persuade them that those interests would best be served by the candidate in question.

The basics of a political race are no less *un*complicated. Where a typical steering committee comes to grief is when the supposed experts in a campaign start arguing over name identification percentages, political registration, money, etc. **Technique becomes confused with goals.**

Basics of Campaigns

There are five basic variables in a political campaign. The first three are considered to be "consumables" in the context of the other two. The three are time, manpower and money. Name identification and party registration in the district are the other two.

Many misunderstandings occur over the use of the latter two. Name identification as a concept gets bandied about too often without ever being defined as to its place in the electoral calculus. The same holds for the party registration in the district.

If everything between two candidates were equal as to time, manpower, and money, and the use of the three variables were equal, then perhaps name identification would bear on the contest. The candidate with the better identification could spend his/her funds in areas designed to maximize voter turnout instead of identifying him/herself. In that case, voter identification of the name would have helped. However, there are practically no contests where "everything else is equal." Consider the two senate races by John Glenn in Ohio. Certainly, after his first ever earth orbiting mission and its national exposure, he had extremely good name I.D. Yet, something as mundane as his slip in the bathtub, which temporarily made him lose his balance and prohibited his campaigning, became much more significant.

An interesting example, which shows that even high name I.D. in and of itself means little, was seen in the 1975 San Francisco mayoral campaign. In a large field of candidates, State Senator Moscone and Supervisor Diane Feinstein were considered to be the leaders. Yet, Judge John Ertola conducted an outstanding name I.D. campaign. Three building contractors put on a political sign crusade for Ertola, erecting over 10,000 signs in the relatively compact city. Observers estimated there were more Ertola signs out than signs for all other candidates combined.[16]

Gene Connel, one of the building contractors behind the Ertola sign campaign, and not a political expert, was quoted in the *San Francisco Chronicle*: "San Francisco is unique for the widespread use of house signs. For some odd reason, it seems there's a direct correlation between the candidate with the most signs and the one who does best on election day."[17] When the votes were counted, it turned out that Ertola had not even been in serious contention against Moscone or Feinstein.

Many examples could show the overrated use of party registration figures, also. On a statewide basis, political pro's like to point out California as a paradox, whereby Democrats outnumbered Republicans three to two, yet Republicans regularly got elected to statewide office.

Or, consider the fifth congressional district in Texas. With overwhelming Democrat registration, it has elected several Republicans to the House, Alan Steelman being one of them. This was in a district which was considered to be 63% central city![18]

It is not only in the South that registration figures can be misleading. Ask Democrat Marvin Durning in the 7th Congressional District in Washington. In the primaries for the two parties for a special election to succeed Democrat Brock Adams, who had resigned to join Jimmy Carter's administration, Democrats had four times the number of voters as Republicans. Clearly, more was involved than the potential vote as indicated by registration on paper. The Democrats had four times the participation. Even before the election, Durning had gone to Washington to line up his committee assignments, to get a head start on representing "his" district.[19] Yet, when the votes were counted on May 17, 1977, Republican State Senator John E. (Jack) Cunningham had won with 54% of the vote, beating Durning.

With so many variables in any election contest, it is extremely dangerous to isolate one variable and put too much weight on it. Back in 1970, Alan L. Otten wrote in the *Wall Street Journal*: "To a man, the experts see party identification and party loyalty dissolving at an increasingly rapid rate; more and more voters identify themselves as independents and boast of ticketsplitting."[20].

The other variables in campaigns lead to just as many misunderstandings on the part of the "cognoscente." The problems stem from people focusing on the availability of a given factor, not its use. This can be seen in races which have concentrated on one particular variable in order to win.

Joe Teasdale, a 36 year old prosecutor of Jackson County, Missouri, ran in the 1972 Democrat primary for governor. He hired as a political consultant, Mat Reese, who was described in the *Wall Street Journal* as: "The best and highest priced professional registration and voter turnout man, anywhere."[21] Later in the same article it said, "This emphasis on grassroots organization makes Mr. Reese all but unique among political campaign consultants . . ." "Manpower" was Mr. Reese's forte. Going into that race, the *Journal* stated that Reese had a 58–14 win/loss record. The campaign was apparently not deficient in other campaign variables, either. Yet, Teasdale lost.

The Fourth District of North Carolina in 1974 saw a well financed race with some of the Republican party's best professionals working to unseat incumbent Democrat Ike Andrews. State Senator Ward Purrington with his own contacts, and the solid help of his prominent wife's family connections, was able to field hundreds of volunteers for campaign projects against Andrews. Purrington was justifiably proud of the large number of enthusiastic volunteers he could mobilize. Yet, Purrington got just 35% of the vote.

Focusing on one variable such as manpower does not give usable knowledge for other campaigns. Even the best and most able of the practitioners of a specific art cannot always make "it" work. Too many other variables and factors are at work. Nowhere is this clearer than in the largely misunderstood area of campaign finance.

The examples of free spending candidates losing the race are legion. John D. Rockefeller IV could not buy his way into the governor's seat in West Virginia in 1972. Richard Ottinger with the backing of his family's U.S. Plywood based fortune could not buy his way into the U.S. Senate in a three-way race in 1970 in New York. James Buckley won the race. John Lindsay in the presidential primary of 1972 in Florida gained notoriety rather than votes in attempting to "buy" a win with massive media advertising. Milton Shapp spent $4 million to try to win the governor's seat in Pennsylvania in 1966 and couldn't do it. Much later in 1994, California Congressman Michael Huffington spent nearly $28 million of his own money and couldn't defeat incumbent Democrat Senator Diane Feinstein in what became the most expensive senate race in history. Feinstein spent about $11 million.

When comparing vote totals in similar types of races, the extreme variability of the "money factor" can be seen. In a 1974 off-year election, Alan Steelman in the Texas 5th District spent $168,457 versus $122,086 for his losing challenger.[22] Steelman won with 28,446 votes compared to 26,190 for the loser. That was over $5.90 per vote. Steelman was the incumbent, yet the district was overwhelmingly registered Democrat.

Democrat incumbent Ike Andrews in the North Carolina 4th District, who had been targeted by the national Republicans in 1974, spent $111,307 versus the challenger's $93,916. Andrews won 62,600 to 33,521.[23] That was about $1.78 per vote.

Clearly, so many variables exist in election contests that to consider any single variable as the "be-all" or "end-all" is unrealistic. Yet, so many times in campaigns, disagreements will arise over the meaning or importance of a single variable.

Usual Flow of a Campaign

Each campaign is unique, of course, in the complexities of the personalities of the people who make up the campaign. Yet, there is often a similarity between "losing" campaigns. This is to say, that the evolution of the campaign in the absence of professionals can often tend to follow similar lines.

Consider a scenario: either the candidate or a key supporter attempts to create a campaign organization. Supporters are enlisted into a loose steering committee. These supporters are usually veterans of many volunteer races with some good business or political contacts. This small grouping will brain storm for names of people who could be enlisted in other areas of the particular district. Out of this nascent organization will arise a nominal "take charge" person, who will act as a manager or coordinator of the efforts.

From this beginning, the campaign rapidly takes on a personality. The political "expertise" of one or two people will often be relied upon as some sort of loose, apparent, consensus develops over what "the issues" ought to be. Even from the beginning, few of the steering committee people are spending much time on the organization, however. The candidate finds he/she is spending more and more time on organization. From the initial enthusiasm of the group, the rote work of searching for supporters and thinking about fund raising takes over.

At about the same time that the initial organization is taking place, other political candidates are in the process of doing the same work. Since party activists are fairly well known through out the area/county from their work on the local central committee, past campaigns, or other community activism, there is much recruiting of the same people. Also, as the organizing tempo picks up, the gossip of the activists starts comparing the efforts of the different groups. In short, a nascent campaign, practically from the beginning, finds itself not only in a projected competition with opposing candidates, but in a competition for resources in its own environment (party, school district, supervisorial, commissioner, etc., district).

As the organizing effort continues, a basic internal tug-of-war in the campaign will start to manifest itself. This becomes a battle over strategy and the use of resources. One solid supporter will push for the purchase of billboards. Another supporter will opt for sniping signs. Yet another supporter wants all the funds-to-be to go into direct mail, etc., etc.

As time goes by, the expectations of the candidate and the organization become disappointed. The candidate is also under the constant press of time in either searching out appearances or preparing for appearances: speeches before an interest group call for research into material for the presentation.

The pressure of a lack of funds draws tempers over the inevitable shortcomings and the compromise in the use of scarce resources. As compromises are made, people will drop away from the campaign because they are either over worked or their ideas are not accepted. Further tensions continue to mount.

In the organization, steering committee meetings, such as they are, start to lose their form. The candidate will see the division of the different sides of the organization over strategy and often withdraw from it by bringing in new people into meetings. This further unsettles the committee as new influences are added.

The result of the campaign problems is that the candidate and the campaign lose, just as most campaigns lose. Unfortunately, the experience is often bitter. A postmortem of the campaign would inevitably show that there had been no centralized goal orientation.

Many candidates, who have fallen into the above trap, would probably admit, after the fact, that they became overwhelmed by the conflicting forces in the campaign. Money is usually the basic scapegoat. Also, the crush of personalities and constant people-problems, both from within and from without, became insuperable.

Few candidates ever realize, after such a failing experience, that they were dealing with at least three campaigns (not two), each co-equal with the other in a community election. The first is the campaign for votes, which is the public face of the campaign. The second is the fundraising campaign, which has the ugliest visage. The third is the "legitimizing" campaign, which seeks support from leadership elements from government, business and interest groups. The third cements the other two together, as will be demonstrated in *Campaigning to Win*. All three need to be initiated and worked together.

The Good News

The good news is that the above scenario of a failed campaign can be short-circuited and transformed into a positive campaign with a solid, forward, direction. The scenario was offered here by way of pointing out the possibilities on the downside. Understanding the existence of these possibilities is a step to the upside.

Peer Levels

At this point a note on "peer" status is necessary. All too many people in their "political ardor" lose touch with "who they are" and "who the people are" with whom they are communicating. What this means is that the "foot soldier" in a campaign does not, all of a sudden, become the social (or otherwise) equal of "generals" in other community organizations or businesses.

A winning election campaign will deal with social levels. Implicitly, most campaigns realize that "it is better to get a country club friend" to solicit funds and other help from a potential donor. This is especially so, when the likely donor is prominent in a particular community. However, a winning campaign needs to remember that the same fact holds true in all areas of the campaign.

It is not snobbery to speak of keeping a cognizance of social levels. The concept is one of empathy. A 53-year-old vice-president of a successful construction firm will feel more comfortable, usually, with his social peers. It is a matter of similar interests. Therefore, the aforementioned vice-president will feel more comfortable in a posh setting talking about fundraising and targeting his friends for support, once his enthusiasm has been aroused. Speaking to the same person about walking a precinct (85% of the time) will leave him cold and embarrassed about how soon to quit the conversation.

That this is not belaboring the obvious, consider the reaction that the typical candidate or steering committee member has upon being questioned by a prominent individual as to how "Mr. Prominent" could help. The first mental image in both the inquiring and answering person's mind is likely to be one of contributing funds. The candidate usually will not ask Mr. Prominent to become a precinct walker, yet feels uncomfortable about asking for funds in this particular situation. Consequently, all too often the offer is sidestepped with a "toss off" comment along the lines of: "Hope you'll tell your friends," or "hope you'll support me to your friends." Much, much, more is possible by remembering status levels.

The correct answer in a "Mr. or Ms. Prominent" situation would be to answer, "Mr. Prominent, I appreciate your interest very much. Could I have your business card? Our campaign chairman, Jim White, would be really interested in your thoughts about our race and the local issues, as am I. Since it's so busy here at this moment, can we call later?" This leaves the door open.

Surmounting the above problems will leave a campaign free to consider other problems.

3

Understanding the System

Most candidates and their steering committees take far too much for granted as to where people and organizations "should" stand in supporting a particular campaign. Much of this problem can stem from confusion about "issues," and where people "should" stand on those issues. However, there is also a haste in campaigns, which does not allow for consideration of certain conditions in human nature.

Considering part of the milieu in which campaigns operate can be helpful. This is because having a "situation-awareness" is the first step to being able to change it, when necessary.

The basic "given" of a campaign is the goal of getting a winning number of votes on election day. Therefore, bearing in mind the sociology of the people, who have the votes to give, is a prime requisite. In other words, it is necessary to "know the course." Winning golf players learn as much of the course on which they are about to play as they can. This is before they hit the first ball.

The discussions, which follow in this chapter, are given by way of lending a context to some of the pressure points, which will be encountered on the campaign trail. These considerations can be considered as reference points, so that a campaign may maintain an even keel in the face of *not* receiving support from

" . . . a sure supporter." Campaigns need to be able to shrug off "negatives," which may arise during the course of the effort.

A campaign needs to consider a district in terms of organizations. These are basic interest groups. Understanding "where political parties are coming from" will save much grief. This holds for other political organizations, as well. Also, the same is true for understanding big business.

Organizations

For the purposes of analyzing a community in an election-context, the first axiom is to consider organizations of people and businesses. The economic and social structure of any community is based on its organizations. Whether the community is urban, suburban, or rural, there are business and social organizations of the people in the area.

Businesses in a community are its foundations. Social organizations of the community have been established to serve other interests. However, to get to most people in a community, find out how they put money in their pocket or what their major spare time avocation is.

Then, of course, there are organizations of organizations. Businesses (defined here as an organization) join with other businesses in chambers of commerce. Churches join with other churches at the ministerial level to form community ministerial organizations. In each case, organizations form to further the interests of the people or organizations in them. The key word, again and again, is "interest."

The strongest organizations for partisan political purposes will be those which mix social and business interests. A chamber of commerce which includes business leaders who are also social leaders is likely to hold a key position in a community. The degree to which it holds a commanding position in the community, with regard to opinion leaders, is the degree to which other organizations (which would have to be found) have not siphoned off these interests.

[In a non-partisan effort, finding the affinity group/meeting area of common interests for a particular field is obvious. In other words, in a school board election race, the PTA (parent teacher association) ("PTSA," etc.) is most likely to be in the position described above (analogously) as held by a strong chamber of commerce.]

Interest Groups

Levels of interest are often important to understanding the power, or lack of it, held by a chamber of commerce or some similar organization. A community with a strong sense of identity (sense of self-interest) will usually have a strong chamber of commerce or community development organization. Then again, the size of the community will often determine the potential for traditional chamber of commerce power to be siphoned off into other organizations. A large community is likely to have several organizations with significant business/social mixes. This could mean a downtown merchants association, a convention and visitors bureau, or others.

Political power, then, in a community will become a function of the organizations in the community. A group (campaign) wishing to influence the politics of a community must determine where the strongest interests are. They must then find the focus of those interests. "Focus of interests" means "the people who regard themselves as the embodiment of the interests" or the "guardians" of such. The details of this process of discovery are covered here in the chapter on a "district inventory."

Consider the uses to which "interest levels" can guide a person. The evolution of political power in many states of the country can be traced by interest levels. The railroad and publishing empires of the latter nineteenth century are cases in point. In hundreds of communities throughout the land, the railroads held political power through the medium of their sharply defined and focused interests in the business sphere. The railroads had money and did not hesitate to use it in the defense and furtherance of their own interests. The legislatures of many states were controlled to alarming degrees by the economic power which the railroads wielded. It was a fairly simple task to find out what the rail interests were and to see how they furthered those interests.

The publishing empires of the same period of time in the country likewise exerted tremendous power. Again, the key, to understanding the uses to which that power would be focused, turned on understanding the particular publisher who had built the power.

These particular political (interest) powers from the past continue to be good laboratory models to refer to, because diffusion of political power had not yet taken place to the degree found in the '1990's. While there are remnants of the empires of the past left, others have now moved in: big-government, big-education, big-environment, big-health-care, and to a lesser extent, big-labor, etc., in addition to big-business or even certain "little-business."

In addition, and rising on the horizon, is the coming "big-ethnic" politics. As the new and huge immigrant communities of the '80's and '90's awaken to their political potential (within the five-year time frame of residence and application for naturalization), big-ethnic politics will muscle many of the other "bigs" off the stage.

The Shift

To a large degree, the success of the U.S. free enterprise system in dispensing its economic benefits has ironically led to the demise of business political barons and promoted other groups from different points of the "interest" compass. Whereas economic power used to be tightly controlled or controllable, enough economic power now lies outside the reach of business, that new influences have arisen. However, the new barons practice no less self-interested politics than the ones they supplanted.

Consider the lines of flow of the political power of "bigness." Were-as classical big-business political power had been largely exerted through the Republican party, the demise of that power was somewhat paralleled by the demise of the historical Republican party in the House of Representatives. The national Republicans controlled the House of Representatives for very few years once FDR's Democrats took over.

Conversely, once FDR had fashioned his coalition of interests against big-business into a winning "critical mass," they, then, became the new "bigs." However, just as the business barons did not represent the average people of their time, neither did the "bigs" of the liberal coalitions. They lost touch with average people, too. Yet, it took until 1994 before the FDR "bigs" would lose control of the House of Representatives (considering 1952 to be an aberration)!

Promise

The "promise" to reach a balance of political interests, such that an average person could in fact be represented politically in the halls of power, is based on coalitions.

It was the building of coalitions of interests, which cracked the political power of the railroads, nineteenth century big business, and nineteenth century publishers. In other words, the size of the parochial interests of those "bigs" was overcome by bringing together enough interest groups in opposition. This is the same road that was taken in the tidal wave change of the 1994 Republican capture of the House of Representatives. Keeping the interest groups together, then, becomes a new task.

It takes a connector to join interest groups to get the voltage for the push. This is the job of the political candidate in his or her campaign.

Political Parties

A note on the interests of the modern day political party, especially the Republican Party in many areas, is appropriate at this point. The "political party establishment" in most counties is that group of people whose interests, economic and otherwise, have led them to get together. These people enjoy politics. They are joined together the same way as any other interest group by their current interests and their past experiences.

There are many bitter former candidates throughout the country who got involved in an election race only to find out that the "party" was not able to automatically come forth with manpower or money to wage a major campaign. It is only political machines, which can *put* a candidate into office. Political parties in most middle class areas are closer to cocktail parties than machine parties.

When understood in the sense of an interest group, then, a political party can be seen to be *attracted* to candidates, often, as opposed to *creating* them. Certainly, there are good county central committees throughout the land, which do a good job of candidate grooming and recruitment. Yet, there is still a difference between a candidate who has said "yes" to an overture to run for an office and the candidate who goes out and demonstrates his/her ability to run effectively.

At the state and federal level, traditional political measurements will tend to override personalities. At the higher levels, the cold numbers of registration, demonstrated campaign effectiveness, and cash in the bank speak the loudest in the competition for resources and attention from the party. In a local party, a personable candidate can sway local attention and some resources by virtue of being personable.

However, even before most candidates are announced and most campaigns put together, the federal, state and local parties will have been targeting certain districts for help. The theory is that more resources put into a smaller number of races will have a larger effect than spreading manpower and money around to token (sacrificial lamb) candidates (running against entrenched incumbents). The problem with such targeting is that in some cases a candidate and campaign will be forsaken strictly because the numbers, based upon party registration, show that the district "can't" be won. At this point the great paradox of the idea that political parties are withering away is confronted by the fact that for a candidate in a party, the party is, for the most part the only game in town. The party does have resources and favors to bestow on chosen candidates. Further, the "chosen" few know who they are. Usually, the "unchosen" do not know that they are not favored until pleas for help fall on deaf ears.

The various party structures from the local, to the state, to the national level, are not isolated from one another. There are people whose job is to know what is going on at all levels. Usually, this is the field director for the area involved. This is a field director either from the state or national party, or from a legislative caucus at the state level, e.g., a state level Republican legislative Caucus. These people are in communication with the local party and certain influential "players," who are looked upon as being "knowledgeable."

A "paper campaign," (token candidate, sacrificial lamb to powerhouse incumbent from the other party), which tries to make contact with the higher party echelons for help is shunted aside by a wall of silence or half answers to questions or pleas for help. The silence can be deafening.

An example of the above, and why it is relevant to a local candidate, is seen in the following. There was a popular Republican congressman on the East Coast, who was in demand as a speaker around the country. He was a celebrity "name." Efforts to contact him on the part of any other than chosen candidates were wholly disregarded. Phone calls were answered by secretaries politely, but the caller was always told that they would be called back. Of course, that never happened. Letters would go unanswered, and mailgrams were of no use either. The only way the wall of silence could be penetrated was through Washington D.C. The key was a speaker's bureau-like group in Washington, which was a national clearinghouse for the multitude of requests on this and other popular congressmen. Only upon the word of the party's local area political director would the machinery in Washington listen to local requests for that congressman to come to the area. There are similar types of formal or informal clearinghouses at the state levels, also.

Again, the way the whole matter of support is approached hangs on the proof of a campaign actually having accomplished positive and meaningful steps. The whole world loves a winner. "Proof of effort" is necessary before even beginning steps can be claimed to be on the road to winning.

Candidate's Conferences

Part of the ceremonial lore of various state parties, and even the national party, is a "candidate's conference." One or more days are jam-packed with conferences, seminars, and speeches on "how to win." Usually, some high-powered professionals, or at least experienced staffers, give good sessions for the candidates. An avid candidate can fill many pages with good notes.

Unfortunately, more information needs to get to most candidates, prior to the conferences. The conferences do in fact usually cover very good material. The conferences do get into what is necessary to win. However, the political expertise at the conferences often cannot be translated into meaningful campaign procedures for an average candidate. This is because the methods and materials, most often touched upon by the professionals making the presentations, will only be within the monetary grasp of those campaigns, which have been "targeted" for party support. That is, the direct mail services, the media specialists, and the polling professionals will only be within the grasp of the "chosen" few. Further, "targeting" has probably taken place well before the conferences. In other words, the campaigns, which need the conferences and the information the most, will likely not be able to use that much of the information which is given. On the other hand, the targeted campaigns in attendance will be getting the time and attention of the professionals in attendance.

A "candidate's conference," thus, becomes a ritual for the staff of the political subdivision which is putting on the conference. Candidates, who have targeted campaigns, will go to the conference in order to cement their positions. Of course, there will be a few candidates, who will be in a contest for one or two slots left open in the ranks of the "chosen," (targeting for party support). These candidates are going to the conference to be looked over, and to make networking contacts. The rest of the candidates, the largest portion, usually, only add to conference attendance figures.

In short, when a "candidate's conference" is convenient and economical, candidates may find something of value in attending. When any sort of sacrifice is necessary to attend such a conference, an evaluation is necessary. The reason for attending should then be for more than the stated reason printed on the top of the program. What *specific* benefits will be obtained by attending a given conference?

"Big Business" Today

Just as businesspeople and businesses continue to be maligned in the popular media, by those who know nothing about business, so too are businesspeople often misunderstood by political candidates. A frequent expression heard from unsuccessful candidates is disappointment in the "business community" for not having supported a campaign.

The mistake, which is being made, is a standard one, which lumps people who are in business together with all others in business. There is no such thing as a "business community" in the sense of a single community of interest along political lines. Each business has its own political community of interest, usually steered closely by its ownership/management. When getting to the level of "big business," local campaigns should be aware that the interests involved might not be locally discernible. "Big business" for purposes, here, means for the most part those companies which have an obvious national and often international prominence: *Fortune* 500, or even *Fortune* 1000 businesses.

Unless a local campaign can identify clear interests on the part of a "big business" firm in a local district, or area, as manifested in the form of prior community involvement, the campaign should not waste too much time in seeking support. Quite simply, a large company is dealing in areas beyond the scope of a local campaign, often beyond a congressional campaign. Consider the following, which will not warm the heart of some conservative activists.

Walter E. Hoadley, Executive Vice President of the Bank of America at the time, made some surprising concessions in a talk he gave to the Commonwealth Club of San Francisco on January 6, 1978. He spoke of the power of environmental groups in their confrontations with business. Then he stated, " . . . business leaders are more and more convinced practical accommodation rather than confrontation is in the public interest as well as their own." He went on to talk of changes in the economy. "We are now in the early stages of another era of massive structural change, which will last for at least five years." One of the changes he spoke of had to do with, " . . . (e)ntrenchment of consumerism and environmentalism in economic, social, and political processes. These protective public "quality of life developments" are here to stay, despite needed, short-term corrections of their impracticalities and inconsistencies."[24]

He went on to cover other "structural changes" such as: "Socialist countries' needs and decisions to lessen economic isolation and seek more Western technology, management skills, products, and credits in order to achieve goals for their people. Principal characteristics of this new normal [sic] are uncertainty, periodic crises, tension, and government interference—but also progress in economic and human welfare."

The speech appeared to be rather innocuous in some quarters, because it acknowledged certain changes which society has seen and some of its problems, even if there was an unsettling tone about it. However, many people were unsettled with his response to the following: "Question: What will be the effect on our economy if France and Italy elect governments composed of a coalition of Socialists and Communists?" Answer: "We'll survive. It's part of the adjustment process."

Again, the subject, here, is the fact that the "business community" does not view political issues all in the same way. "Accommodations" do take place. There are "shifts."

A philosophical enunciation of a "shift" was given in the September 1975 issue of *Fortune* magazine. An article was headlined: "Business Needs a Different Political Stance," was written by a Max Ways. A "subhead" was: "Their present position casts businessmen as doctrinaire conservatives and inhibits them from making the contribution to public life that they're capable of." The summation of the article in the "*Fortune*'s Wheel" covered the article well: "Most U.S. businessmen seem to have little trouble finding their 'natural' place in the conventional political spectrum . . . They position themselves off there to the right, and they love those speeches denouncing government interference with business . . . A more important difficulty is that this conservative stance isolates business from the political process. By automatically opposing all regulation and all governmental social programs, businessmen forgo the opportunity to help the American public distinguish between workable and unworkable programs. That kind of contribution might recapture for business some of the constructive political influence it had in the past." The article finished with the following sentence: "It is by showing a willingness to cooperate with the American people in the management of change that business may regain the political influence it once had."

The above are not isolated examples. David Finn, chairman of the board of Ruder & Finn, a public relations firm in New York, did an article for the *New York Times* called, "Human Values and Businessmen." The first sentence stated the article's position: "Business credibility might improve if more executives were willing to admit—even to themselves—that the obligation to pay adequate attention to public needs has not yet become one of the requisites of sound management."[25]

Such a development of a rationale for business to rethink its stance has had other consequences. Avon, AT&T, IBM, McDonald's and Proctor and Gamble sponsored a "Lesbian Guide."[26] Avon Products Corporation contributed $2,000.00 to the pro-ERA constitutional amendment campaign, when that fight was still going on in New York state in 1975.

The key point is that a "business" point of view or a "business position" needs to be examined closely before a campaign can work with such an idea, when searching for support from business.

So What

In summary, a campaign needs to try to appeal to the interests of the people and organizations in its district. There are too many people and organizations with which to work, however, to let the denial of support from any particular person or interest group cast a pall over a campaign. Since people like winners, a political campaign, which goes about its work and becomes a force in its own right, will often see support, which was denied earlier in a campaign, come over to the campaign at a later time.

4

Literature on Campaigns

Literature in the popular press about "politics" is not insignificant. There is a fascination on the part of the public and the media with winning (and losing) politicians and hotly contested "issues," which come to a vote. This is often reflected by the popularity of "insiders" works, such as the series, "The Making of the President," by Theodore H. White. From time to time even the mechanics of campaigns get studied, as in the *Wall Street Journal* article, " A Modern Machine: How Savvy Matt Reese, A Political Consultant, Gets Out Winning Vote." (March 23, 1972)

However, anyone trying to divine the "stuff" of campaigns, would not be well served by saving a file of *Time* magazine, or *U.S. News & World Report*, or others, clippings on campaign mechanics. Such a collection of ditties and vignettes would be more confusing than enlightening.

Unfortunately, the same holds true for much of the published specific literature on mechanics, the books on political campaigns. The basic problem with so many works is that they either overshoot or undershoot their mark, if in fact they state what their mark is. A step further is the example of stating one's focus and completely missing the target. Consider, for example, the "focus" given by political scientist Robert Agranoff in his book,

Management of Election Campaigns. He states in his introduction that the material in this book is designed to guide a campaign " . . . from the small community election to national office elections, high or low visibility contests, small and large budgets, primary or general elections."[27] This would seem to be akin to writing a book, *"The Compleat Seaman's Manual: From Rowboats to Aircraft Carriers."*

A closer look at two interesting books on campaign techniques is instructive. Both books are valuable for their insights, but they come from opposite ends of a spectrum. They are Steven C. Shadegg's work, *How to Win an Election,* and Hal Evry's book, *The Selling of a Candidate."*

Shadegg's experience as a seasoned campaign tactician is thoroughly evident in his work. His book is written from the point of view of a campaign manager and covers just about all areas that major campaigns encompass. Shadegg presents some material with regard to candidates, but the thrust of the work is tactical. Basic district analysis is given, studies on undecided and indifferent voters are presented, and mass communication techniques are screened.

Shadegg's material on the use of T.V., radio, and direct mail is good. His instructions on the establishment of what he calls "the cell group," a group of people prominent in their communities, are excellent. His communication with the reader as to the size and magnitude of the task of garnering large vote totals is well done, also.

However, Shadegg's "war stories" throughout the book undermine much of his carefully laidout work for establishing a well rounded tactically sound campaign. The reader is impressed with the research work, issue handling, volunteer direction, and media orchestration required to beat the opposition. However, a sense of fatalism is developed by the end of the book in view of many references to the "one tactic" that "put it over." For example, "one direct mail piece that devastated the opposition," is covered in the book. "Burma Shave signs that "one-upped" the other side" are presented. "Dear friends" postcards, which carried another campaign over the top, are recounted with relish. Many other examples such as an outstanding radio spot or a campaign photograph with "just the right emphasis on the angular qualities of the candidate's jaw" are given.

What impresses the reader seeking direction for campaigning is the apparent capriciousness of the Fates, whereby in a high-priced, well-organized, professionally run campaign, one little item can make or break the whole effort. As Shadegg says, "If in our journey into the realities of political campaigning, you may have gained the impression that this political jungle is a world of make-believe where the tricks of the trade can produce victory, put aside that misconception."[28] Unfortunately, the reader is left with exactly that impression.

Another criticism, which holds true for most works such as Shadegg's book, is that the focus of the book is on the very group of campaigns that don't need such a book. Campaigns at the state level which are considered to be "real" races, and which will spend large sums of money, are hiring professionals in their fields and using professional campaign advisors. A senate or gubernatorial race which needed to read a book on campaign technique would be out of the contest before it even began. Similarly, a set-piece battle between Republicans and Democrats in a swing congressional or assembly district will draw vast sums of money and political expertise. In a different vein, a Howard Hughes, Warren Buffet, or even Bill Gates would not need to read a book called, *Think & Grow Rich!*[29]

In summary, Shadegg's book is a good contribution to campaign literature. It breaks ground for an understanding of traditional campaign concepts and techniques. Yet, much more is needed for nonprofessionals in campaigning than is offered in the book.

A nontraditional approach to campaigns, with a highly irreverent tone to the business of winning elections, is Hal Evry's book, *The Selling of a Candidate.*"[30] Party registration, name identification, and public speaking ability are not even considered as relevent items to a campaign or candidate, according to Evry's political calculus.

An article in *Life* magazine in June 1966 carried much of Evry's philosophy for campaigns as presented in his book. The article carried three qualifications that Evry demanded in a candidate, before Evry would direct the candidate's campaign. The first was cash on the barrelhead for Evry's public relations firm. Second, the candidate needed to present the appearance of a character consistent with what Evry called the "code of the great middle cluster of normality." Third, the candidate needed to score at least 120 on the Stanford-Binet intelligence test. The idea behind the intelligence test was so that the candidate could understand Evry's prohibitions of speeches and other classical "campaigning."

What was left out of the *Life* article and Evry's book, was any concern for volunteer organizations, opposition research, or handling of "issues." Advertising is presented in the book as the "open-sesame" to the Evry approach to campaigns. The *Life* article quoted Evry on advertising. "'Open any magazine,' says Evry. 'Look at the ad pages. People are paying tens of thousands of dollars for these pages. They can't afford to make mistakes. What do you see on these pages? Do you see long, involved fancy logical arguments? Never. You see something that grabs your attention and you see a good slogan—a good simple, primitive, repetitive slogan. That's what gets 'em.'"

Perhaps the best contribution to the science of vote gathering by Evry was his approach to understanding the average voter. Evry would probably not disagree if his approach to campaigning were likened to that of George Washington Plunkitt of Tammany Hall, who said, "I don't trouble them with political arguments. I just study human nature and act accordingly.'"

The trouble with the Evry approach to campaigning can be likened to Minerva springing full grown from the brow of Jupiter. A candidate who would use Evry's approach to campaigning would need to be fully financed from the beginning of the campaign.

The Evry book is good. It makes a valuable contribution to the literature on campaigning, also, because it forces a rethinking on so much classical and traditional political lore. For example, compare the following views.

Political scientist Robert Agranoff says, "One of the most vital, continuous, inexpensive, and potentially effective public-relations techniques is door to door campaigning by the candidate."[32] Not so, according to Evry, who says, "Every book on politics urges candidates to get out and ring doorbells, shake hands, and meet the public. Every book on politics is wrong about this. Engaging in such activity is not only tiring, but useless as well."[33].

There are many other works on campaigning. The political science section in a college book store is a smorgasbord of such works. However, in too many cases the works deal with large district or state level campaigns. In many cases, the books miss the mark by attempting to deal with the minutia of campaigns. Chapters on "how to be a good advance man" have no applicability to the vast majority of campaigns in congressional-sized races or smaller. Chapters, which give examples of regret letters for canceling a speaking engagement, are a waste of space. Even an in-depth exposition of press conferences has little relevance for most campaigns.

Of course, details on news release writing, fundraising dinners, and opposition research are important. However, a better source for basic campaign nuts and bolts is the material put out by the political parties themselves. National political parties and state political parties gather and generate large amounts of "how to" materials. Furthermore, they constantly revise the materials in new formats.

The national parties usually release their materials through their "candidates conferences" and "practical politics" conferences. The same holds true for state parties. Smaller state parties, which do not generate their own materials, often rely on larger states and the national parties. A person wishing to obtain materials regarding their local area need only ask their local or state level headquarters in the state captital.

One of the best examples of this type of material was the official manual of the Republican National Committee, when Senator Bob Dole of Kansas was the chairman. The manual was called "Campaign Seminars" with ten self-contained pamphlets. The subjects covered were: campaign organization, fund raising, mobilizing manpower, media advertising, media relations, campaign graphics, opposition research, telephone boiler rooms, fundraising dinners, and budgeting.

Each section of the manual had examples and explanations in the form of checklists for the different techniques covered. For example, the pamphlet on campaign organization had four pages of sample organization charts with lines of responsibility, etc. The pamphlet on media relations had examples of news releases complete with notes in the margins explaining the "why" and "wherefore's" of a release. In short, the manual covered every technique, which campaigns find necessary to further their ends.

Examples of various state party's campaign manuals are abundant. One such manual on the East coast is the "1974 Legislative Campaign Seminar" printed by the North Carolina Republican Party, which was printed expressly for its meeting that year at the Hilton Inn in Raleigh. The manual had five sections: campaign organization, fund raising, campaign finance law, the press kit, and 1974 campaign issues.

Out on the West Coast the same year, the Republican State Central Committee of California published its manual for its statewide seminars, "The Republican Campaign Primer." The Primer's table of contents had sections on professional management, precincts, headquarters, telephone banks, publicity, fundraising, direct mail, and campaign organization.

Aside from material prepared for specific seminars and conferences, some extremely good manuals on key campaign techniques exist. The Republican National Committee published a 59 page work by Mary Ellen Miller which was titled, "Boiler Room Operation." Some years ago, the same party published a little 21 page pamphlet called "The GOP Precinct Leaders' Manual."

Other examples of basic works come from California. A manual called "Building a Productive Organization" had four sections: "building your precinct organization," volunteer recruitment, party auxiliaries and special voter groups. A very good pamphlet called "What you've always wanted to know about fundraising—but didn't know whom to ask" gave checklists for just about any detail of fund-raising imaginable.

As a matter of fact, the California Republican Party has been a resource party for many state parties, which reproduce the California work. The point of the various examples given above is that the major parties are fountains of materials for basic works. Also, interest groups put out material, which is worthwhile. The Libertarian party published "Political Action Bulletins." It was a twelve chapter booklet on political campaign techniques written specifically for Libertarian candidates.

An interesting round robin illustration of the constant flow of materials was seen in a booklet, which was published by the California Republicans called, "Building for Victory." The booklet described the extremely effective volunteer precinct organization get-out-the-vote effort produced by the Bob Kasten organization in Wisconsin. According to Jacqueline Irby of the Republican National Committee in a seminar at the California Spring Republican Convention in 1978, it was some basic California materials from the early 1960's, which were used as a basis for the Kasten plan! The Kasten plan worked so well that it was presented at the 1974 Conservative Political Action Conference in Washington D.C. As word spread about the effectiveness of the Kasten plan, the Committee for the Survival of a Free Congress (CSFC) printed up a booklet on the plan. In 1977 the California Republicans reproduced the CSFC booklet.

Yet other areas produce campaign organizational "how to" literature. The weekly conservative newspaper, *Human Events*, offered a pamphlet called, "Everything You Should Know About Practical Politics." *Human Events* continues, yearly, to publish a booklet called, *"The Conservative Action Guide."* [For more information on this publication, call 1–800–787–7557] First printed in 1975, it has gone through ten editions, with two having been done in 1995. The Young Republican National Federation published a worthwhile looseleaf book called, "Youth Campaign Source Book." In a number of states the local telephone company has sponsored nonpartisan seminars on citizen involvement in the campaign process.

It becomes obvious that once a person gets attuned to looking for campaign materials, much is available. However, the same problem as mentioned above regarding the books on campaigns holds true. By erecting so many trees of technique, the forest of campaigns gets obscured. Even an organization which had two years to collect and study campaign technique would still be in the position of having to get its candidate in agreement with the campaign manager and/or steering committee as to what the basic campaign strategy would be.

A Shadegg approach to a campaign could become characterized in the mind of a reader as being a campaign of projects, with many projects orchestrated by project leaders led by a campaign manager. The Evry approach would focus on the mass media. Matt Reese, the political consultant written up by the *Wall Street Journal*, put his emphasis on grass roots organizations. Yet another political consultant covered in the media, David Garth, was quoted almost diametrically opposed to the Evry approach. *Advertising Age* quoted Mr. Garth as saying that people have become "more sophisticated in the reasons they vote for candidates. They want more issues, more facts. You'd have a very difficult time doing a campaign with a guy with no issues and no background."[34]

The problem remains after all the candidates' seminars, campaign managers and coordinators seminars, and various smorgasbords of technique and approaches. As a campaign becomes embodied in bodies sitting around a table discussing "how to win," the various "experts" get their ego entwined with "their" approach. In exasperation, campaigns often get broken up, or compromised, into fiefdoms with petty "warlords," who "know" their political "ground" better than anyone else. "Middletown will be handled by Mary Jones her way. Jones County will be handled by Bill Smith his way, etc . . ." A campaign, then, finds itself stroking the egos of the various "experts" whose credentials derive often from having been a member of the county party for twenty years, or from having been elected to the board of directors of a local political club. Further, "nice" campaign plans produced for the edification of prospective contributors, gather dust in a drawer somewhere, having succumbed to the "realities" of "this particular" district.

After a losing campaign, when the smoke has cleared, various themes often become "obvious" in retrospect. The first is usually money. A finance chairman who was picked for his "access" to money or people with money, didn't do his job. Or, the campaign manager who had lined up several "sure fire" vote getting projects, got bogged down in one or two of the projects. This led to letting even organizational basics slip by, such as not getting out what literature was available. Third, the candidate had become more or less estranged from the power struggles within his/her own campaign organization and careened back and forth from one advisor to another, looking for a magic talisman.

The answer to the problems from too many typical losing campaigns is generally never addressed. Or, if it is, it is shrugged off. Simply, and simplistically, the answer is found in the word "strategy" and what it means.

That this is *not* as obvious as it might appear, consider the following comments on the subject of a "strategy" for campaigns. Shadegg said: "The experienced campaign manager will devise his strategy to sharpen the differences between his candidate and the opponent."[35] Furthermore, while Shadegg lists a campaign strategy as number six in his list of 20 important items for an election timetable, the word is not used again. Number nine in the list says: "Assemble the full team and start them thinking about the candidate, about his opponent and about the issues."[36] This is the proper area for strategic planning.

The Republican National Committee Campaign Management College manual for 1973 defined "campaign strategy" as "a set or series of objectives whose achievement maximizes the probability of attaining 50% plus 1 of the total votes cast in any specific election." The same manual defined "campaign plan" as "a program of specific activities designed to achieve the campaign's strategic objectives."

A campaign strategy must derive from specific research regarding the district, and a core strategy must include "issues," organization, and fundraising in an integrated system. The three cannot be run as separate projects.

All of this becomes apparent through the process of doing a district and vote "inventory."

5

District Inventory

A campaign has already been defined as a set of actions by a group of people in pursuit of a specific objective. However, another definition is more instructive and simpler. **A campaign is a marshaling of the available forces in a district to bring about a desired result.** "Forces" means people and their organizations. Before the forces can be marshaled, they must be identified. The usefulness of such a definition is that it gives a focus to a campaign that most campaigns lack.

The systematic identification of available people, organizations, and businesses must be the foundation rock of any campaign. Most campaigns pay lip service to the idea, but few follow through with a thorough district economic analysis and distribution-of-influence analysis. A less formidable name for such a task is to call it simply, a district inventory.

The Study

A district inventory is a compilation of the geographic, business, and social "foci" of the people in the district. Since a political campaign needs to be interested in people who are in positions to influence others, such people need to be systematically identified as to their position, how they may be met, and what their interests are. An inventory will identify such people by their position and the inventory will identify people who are in a position to introduce the campaign to the people which are focused upon.

Because elections come around every two years, there is usually a basic foundation of information available as to political contributors to past campaigns, past campaign workers, and activists. Certain businesspeople over the years become identified with a party and a viewpoint. These people are "approachable" by virtue of their labelling and should be considered as basic resource people. This is not for instant contributions of time or money, but as "orientation persons."

An Aside on Support People

One aside, here, is appropriate. In many campaigns the chief people involved, and the candidate, will often be miffed by a "lack of support" from Mr. "Important." The prevailing attitude is that because Mr. "I". is a Republican, or whatever, that he should automatically step forth, forthwith, offering time and money to the current standard bearers. Nothing could be further from reality. A political label will many times get a door opened, or lead to access to a person, but that is all. It is up to the campaign to get the interest of the individual involved. The generic terms of "Christian," "Jew," "Rotarian," "Mason," "Elk," etc., indicate a *potential* community of interest, only. In no case do individuals under a given umbrella take the generic term to mean that they embrace all other individuals who use the term. Southern Baptists and Catholics both call themselves Christians, but the similarities between them do not necessarily continue.

Beginning the District Inventory

A district inventory will be divided into geographical units, usually by city, but in any case, by region. A congressional district with five cities in it will have a loose leaf notebook with a division for each city or region. Each region will then be inventoried.

One way to begin the inventory is to use the yellow pages of the phone book, if the region to be covered is the predominant area listed in the pages. Simply list each major heading for businesses and professions. That a given type of business is usually the backbone of an area is obvious, but most people are unaware of the scope of the ancillary businesses to a predominant business. This is especially important in an area where a major "big business" (eg., Fortune 500 listed company) is the dominant firm in a given district. In all too many cases, candidates from the level of those running for Congress to local hospital boards, are ignored by the large firms. This is especially so in a district with an incumbent. Even in a district represented by a flaming radical, companies will in many cases have made their "peace" with the politician along the lines of "live and let live."

Through the inventorying process, it will be seen that the lack of support from one area can often be more than made up in other areas.

Most of the businesses extracted from the yellow pages will fit under the following headings:

> Agribusiness
> Banking
> Communications/media
> Construction
> Fuel, energy
> Insurance
> Labor
> Manufacturing
> Professions
> Real Estate
> Restaurants
> Retail Trade
> Service Industry:

Phones, lights, gasoline, travel, TV repair, etc
Transportation
Wholesale trade

With such a basic inventory, a flow of funds of the area can be worked out. In a large manufacturing plant area, the pay roll of the manufacturer is obviously the economic basis of the region. However, the suppliers to the manufacturer are important often in their own right, etc. Again, the object of such an exercise is to see where the pressure points are and who the person is who controls a given point.

With this basic intelligence, a campaign can then approach knowledgeable people in the area—each area. The knowledgeable people could be from the local chamber of commerce. In every chamber of commerce there will be a president, a past president, an executive director or someone who will be sympathetic to the aims of a legitimate candidate and his legitimate organization. If a chamber of commerce has been supplanted by some other entity, whatever the organization is, it will have people who are knowledgeable about the economy of the area and who various "individuals of stature" are.

Such a study will lead to civic and community clubs as a source for finding influential people. For example, the local Rotary Club will usually have many "movers and shakers" from the community. Then, through such clubs or organizations, many times, persons, willing to make introductions, can be found. Such people can be found from their having been on contributors lists, etc. The membership of the influential civic organizations are often quite useful, too.

Chambers of commerce and community organizations are not magic talismans, however. They are a beginning. After some preliminary contacts, it will soon be discovered that there are many, many organizations of different professions, businesses, and interest groups, which hardly ever hit the pages of newspapers, yet, which have made it their duty to understand and be able to influence various economic and political levers of pressure.

Refer to the list of categories uncovered when doing the district inventory. "Construction" is a likely category in most districts. The construction industry is often one of the most important. The construction industry has a direct interface with government, because of government regulations on building. The industry is constantly in contact with government at many levels in the course of different projects.

A campaign making its inventory of construction firms and their owners-presidents-managers must also search out various construction based organizations. These are the organizations which construction specialties have formed to look after their own interests. Electrical contractors will usually have an electrical contractors organization, whose task is to keep the members informed of current laws and practices emanating from state, county and local levels. Such an organization will usually have a staff somewhere which reports to the construction members. This staff is in the position of knowing relevant governmental impacts on its members. The staff will also know who the most active members of the industry are in the local district.

A campaign organization does itself a major disservice by not seeking out the knowledge that such an organization can, *if it chooses*, give. The information need not come direct from the organization; it can come from a particular member, eg., electrical contractor, who is sympathetic to the campaign.

This is just one example. There are as many types of such organizations as there are contractors. All such organizations must by their nature be non-partisan. However, sympathetic people can provide information, leads, and later, funds.

The same holds true for various professions. There are national and quite often state organizations of each type of specialist in medicine. Doctors in a political district can provide a campaign with considerable help in making influential contacts aside from fund raising.

Enlisting Support

The goal of a district inventory is to find a person who will become an activist for the campaign from each business, profession, or field. This person then helps the campaign by his or her knowledge of who other influential people are. The activist will send letters of support to people in his/her field. Such letters will ask for support and recognition first. Only later are funds solicited.

The purpose of the activists for a campaign is to magnify its activities. Not only does a campaign not have specialized knowledge, but it does not have the resources or credibility in the field of an activist. A campaign will ask an activist to send out letters on his/her own letterhead asking for recognition of the campaign. An activist, under the right circumstances, can even become the chair of a letterhead organization, "Electrical Contractors for Jones," which does nothing more than send out letters of support and later solicit funds. The letters can be sent out all at once, or sent in a steady flow of ten letters per week for X-number of weeks. This all depends on the commitment of the activist.

In the course of building the district inventory and in the course of recruiting activists from the lists arising from the inventory process, certain highly influential people will have their name arise several times over. To the degree that these people are in fact real political factors and can in fact lend strength to the campaign, then these people must be courted for their support.

One of the best ways to court such a person is to get a supporter who knows him/her to take the candidate and the influential person to lunch. A very clear understanding must be made that no financial support will be solicited at this meeting. The session is purely for purposes of letting the influential person meet the candidate. Such a meeting should be followed up with a note from the candidate, which says that the candidate was pleased to meet the man/woman and that the candidate appreciated the information and views that Mr./Ms. Influential spoke of during the lunch. (A thank-you note to the supporter who bought the lunch goes without saying.) The campaign would then make a reminder to follow up on what Mr. Influential had indicated his interests were. With a newsclipping from a newspaper or such, the campaign would send a note to Mr. Influential "for your interest." A note from the supporter, who arranged the lunch, to "Influential" telling him that the campaign is coming along nicely will be of help also.

If the courting of these influential people is done properly, some of them will in fact ask how they can help. This is the pay off. These influential people should be asked, first, to send letters of support to people whom they know to be influential, also. If Mr./Ms. Influential's secretary can do a mail-merge on the office computer (on personal or corporate stationery), then asking for 100 letters is no big deal. Extending the chain of the highest influential people, the offer of support can be translated into another lunch with another influential person.

Influential people will have been chosen for their influence. Consider the manager of a medium sized manufacturing plant, who by his involvement in many community affairs has become widely known and highly regarded. The manufacturing plant has suppliers of many different articles. The manager could send a note of support to the principal people who supply the plant. Also, the plant makes use of different professionals. There are legal services supplied, medical services supplied, accounting services supplied, large insurance needs met, etc. The manager of the plant who has offered to help can drop a note of support in the mail to each of these suppliers. Also, the man has personal suppliers of his own needs: doctors, lawyers, tax accountants, insurance agents, etc. Further, the organization memberships of the man are targets. A note to the president of the Rotary Club, the country club, etc. would be of significant help. The campaign in a sense has recruited the influential person's secretary, postage, and influence lists, in the ever widening circles of campaign influence. In this manner, a campaign multiplies itself beyond the limits of "campaign disclosure laws."

Certain obvious constraints become apparent in the flow of this line of endeavor for the campaign and the candidate. There are narrow limits on the time availability of the candidate, the number of supporters who are willing to pick up the tab for lunches, and the ability of the campaign staff to follow through with the secretarial requirements of all the different "courting notes." Also, in a congressional district there are usually several different cities or regions with many different widely influential people. However, a campaign's political arithmetic will provide the calculus as to weighting the degree of time, effort, and other resources used in the pursuit of this type of endeavor. Potential votes and funds-availability are the two variables with the highest degree of relevance. A city with 25% of the potential vote for the candidate should receive about the same amount of campaign resource allocation. With 60 days left in the campaign, that city should receive about 15 days. The district inventory of that city obviously cannot bend the candidate or the campaign to devote much more than the 25% of resources. However, the great utility of an inventory is that priorities can be readily observed or "kept up with."

Also included in a district inventory is the governmental inventory of the city or area. Every elected official who would be remotely favorable to the candidate, must be listed and contacted in some way. These people, by holding office, are in contact with many people. A very real calculation must be made as to the jealousies and potential empires of these office holders when allocating time to seeking the person's support. In some cases a sitting congressman can be of considerable help to a state legislative candidate, when the congressman can see some benefit to him/herself in helping the other candidate. However, the representative has his or her own race, their own need for funds, and their own staff limitations. Usually, a county commissioner/supervisor who is not up for re-election or a state senator not up for re-election is the best source of potential "current office holder help." However, they must be asked for help. The rule of self interest, again, on the part of the office holder is a primary calculation.

The development of a governmental inventory for the different areas will spotlight several additional areas for potential support. As the campaign lists the current members of hospital boards, sanitary districts, city councils, etc., past candidates for these posts will also be potential targets for asking for support.

Religious and educational interests in the district should also be considered in the district inventory. The goals of this particular search will probably be somewhat limited when compared to the other categories, but these groups have some potential. A minister willing to actively help, could be of help in his particular sphere.

The boards of trustees of community colleges can be good for recruiting support. Many times the trustees are successful community oriented businesspeople or educators with wide contacts of their own.

It is only by such inventorying that a campaign will be able to identify the interests of the district. A district is made up of its people. Further, those people have channeled their interests. The person who would represent the district must not only know the interests, but the people who have those interests.

A word of caution, however, is important. There are "old war horses" out there. Many of them have fought losing battles for years, and have become somewhat jaded in their outlook on the possibilities of winning in their districts. Their negativism comes from batting their head against the same wall for so many years. The approaches offered here are not orthodox "organize the precincts." Many campaigns will likely encounter many "experts" who will say that the district is un-winnable. However, when this is heard, consider the source. Unfortunately, these people may have gained a vested interest in losing. After all, they have tried and tried and not been successful. Someone likely to be successful, could "embarrass" what were previous "losers ."

The best campaign supporter is the one with enthusiasm. If old political warhorses of the district have lost their enthusiasm, a campaign needs to search elsewhere for support. Once a winning campaign is developed, the warhorses will often come along with the band-wagon, however.

This identification by the campaign of the influence centers of the district should be done on an equal time and resource basis along with the development of a massvote-solicitation campaign. This is in fact *the* critical factor in the effectiveness of the campaign. As has been shown in other sections of this work, name I.D. will not win a race. Mass media alone will not win a race. A critical variable is acceptance by the people in the district. Opinion leaders of the community do in fact exert influence, because they are known in the community as people who have community interests in mind. Many political activists are asked, by people who know that the activist is politically active, who should be voted for. Just as an activist gets questions like this, the man or woman of influence in the community will influence many, many votes. The questioner does not have the interest to search out the necessary information. Two days before an election many people will ask, "who is Mr. Influence going to vote for in the Jones race?" The premise of the question is: "I don't care about such a race. It holds no interest for me. However, I know that Mr. Influence does care about it. Therefore, what is good enough for him is good enough for me. After-all, I am a patriotic citizen and do want to exercise my right to vote and to understand what I'm voting for. Mr. Influence will show me."

The other side of the same coin is the mass media campaign from which people see a name often enough to ask, toward the end of the campaign, if "so-and-so is 'any good'." They will ask someone they believe pays attention to such matters. If that "someone" does not know, very little has been gained by the campaign. People are not stupid and they are largely fair. They know that a race is two sided. The best campaign going is going to encounter resistance due to the partiality of the campaign. Many people will decide in favor of a candidate only after they have had a reinforcing opinion which confirms their partisanship. Most candidates for office are familiar with the question, "who are you running against?" All the puffery possible will not convince a voter, until that voter has had a chance to ask someone else for their opinion, someone whom they hold in political regard.

A very interesting demonstration of the power of "the other person" was used by an incumbent congressman in a re-election drive against a conservative candidate, who was a war hero. The challenger had impugned the congressman's record on national defense positions. The attack was mounted using standard newsreleases and paid advertisements, which is standard political fare.

The day before the election, the congressman ran the following ad in the local daily newspaper: "Veterans for 'Jones." "He's Working For Us" was the headline. The copy in the ad mentioned the congressman's military record and stated that he " . . . continues to be dedicated to the service of his country, his community, his church and always to his fellow citizens. We are veterans from all ranks, private to major general, whose service to our county spans the period from World War I through Vietnam. We recognize Congressman 'Jones' distinguished military service and his continuing interest in veteran's needs and problems. We also appreciate the experience and understanding he brings to bear on the problems of our Congressional District."[37] The ad listed nearly 600 names surrounding the copy in the half page listing. Such an ad washed out thousands of dollars of "paid political announcements" on the part of the challenger with the exceptionally strong power of personal endorsements. Just about everyone who had lived in the district for any period of time knew many of the names on the listing.

A campaign deals in large numbers of votes. However, there

is a person behind each vote. The next task of a campaign is to identify where the mass of votes lies in order to make person to person contact with those votes.

A campaign strategy must derive from specific research regarding the district, and a core strategy must include "issues," organization, and fundraising in an integrated system. The three cannot be run as separate projects.

All of this becomes apparent through the process of doing a district and vote "inventory."

6

Vote Inventory

Voting analysis of a district need not be esoteric or painful "spreadsheet type" work. It has one goal: to find the best areas for finding the necessary votes to win. The analysis is done on the basis of past voting behavior and some socio-economic factors.

In a partisan race, when a person looks for the best areas in which to get votes, it means that the potential of a precinct to change votes from one party to another is being probed. Two extremes make the point. If a precinct votes about 65% for the Republicans all the time, the chances of squeezing significantly more Republican votes out of that precinct are less than a precinct which has given from 45% to 55% to the Republicans over some elections. The point is one of resources. The chances of hitting a responsive chord with one hundred contacts of potential voters are greater in a swing precinct than in a 65% precinct. This is because in a high percentage precinct most of the votes have been spoken for.

The same holds true in a high percentage precinct for the opposition. Since most of the votes have been garnered by the other side, the chances are lessened that people could be contacted who would be responsive to appeals for votes.

[To test the ideas presented in this chapter, the reader is

guided to the appendix in this work, which shows actual vote totals for several different levels of representation from a real congressional district in 1974 and then again in 1992.]

Base Vote

There is a natural constituency for each party which makes up a base vote in each precinct and each political district. [While a little more complicated to analyze, the same holds true in non-partisan races.] A "base vote" is cast for the party and not the candidate. Therefore, any candidate running will most likely start from that base.

To estimate a base vote for a precinct, find the worst race run by a candidate from the party. The difference in percentage of total vote won in the poor race can be subtracted from the best race run in the precinct. This difference in percentages is the swing percentage. The smaller the percentage change from low to high, the less responsive the precinct would appear to be to campaigning. Conversely, the greater the percentage change, the better the precinct is for campaigning.

For example, consider a state legislative race four years earlier where the Republican candidate was not considered to be a threat to the Democrat. Such a race probably expended very little meaningful effort. If the Republican got 30% of the vote, that is likely to be a Republican base vote. (Thirty percent of the electorate votes for the Republican, no matter who it is.) If at the same time a popular candidate won the U.S. Senate seat for the Republicans with 60% of the vote in that precinct, there has been a swing of 30% in the vote. This would be a fertile field in which to seek out votes for a Republican candidate.

Prioritizing

On the other hand, if the percentage swing from low race to high race was small, the likelihood of getting more votes out of that precinct is considerably less. From the point of view of expending campaign resources in campaigning, precincts with an average base vote (considering the district) and a high swing percentage are the best targets. The least fertile fields are 1. the heart of the enemy's territory (his/her highest base vote) and 2. the heart of your support (your highest base vote). In either case, expending much effort in those precincts is least likely to generate more votes out of the territory.

In cases where it is not readily apparent which are the high potential swing vote precincts, there is a method for generating a hierarchy of precincts. To list precincts in order of priority (the priority to use for searching out more votes) multiply the percentage swing vote times the actual numbers of votes swung from the high vote total race compared to the low vote total race.

For example, in a precinct which had swung 25% from the low candidate race to the high candidate race, and which had seen the high candidate get 100 more votes than the low, the number derived is a gauge of "vote potential."

[Obviously, the higher the percentage of votes switched, and the higher the absolute numbers of votes switched, the greater the potential switch, and the better an area to work in. A 25%-swing-and-100 plus-votes-precinct gets a number of 25 (25% times 100). A precinct which had a 20% swing and a switch of 80 votes gets a number of 16 (20% times 80).

In this manner, a numerical hierarchy of precincts can be established relatively quickly. This is a basic requirement for establishing priorities of precincts.]

The socio-economic factors in the political inventory will shade the prioritization of the precincts by the accessibility of the precinct. Where two precincts had the same vote potential number, the suburban precinct, which was more compact than the rural precinct, would rate higher for purposes of posting signs or candidate door to door walking. There would be no difference for mailing purposes.

When the prioritization project has been completed, posting

the results on a precinct map of the district will become instructive. Shading the high priority precincts or coloring them, will likely give a very interesting "feel" as to where to get the votes.

The time for a nicely reasoned and dispassionate analysis for prioritization purposes is available only before the heat of the battle. It is necessary to know where to spend money, time and manpower before they become available.

The goal of the potential vote analysis is to find the votes that would total a winning number, obviously. A projection of a winning number of votes is necessary in order to be able to set vote goals for the precincts.

Calculating a probable winning vote total can be done starting from previous races in the district during the same type of election years, i.e., presidential election years ("on-year") or non-presidential election years ("off-year"). Comparing total votes to total registration over several past elections will give a likely bracket of a high turnout for the district and also a low turnout. Looking at hotly contested races' vote totals will also help. In addition, it is important to consider the possibilities of highly emotional election contests, which could influence voter turnout, e.g., a referendum on abortion rights or such. At any rate, considering past vote statistics will give a good idea of what a winning total might be for the district and race involved.

It then becomes necessary to find the votes in the precincts starting with the highest vote potential precincts and working down the list. It will become readily apparent in searching for a winning number of votes that party lines will most probably have to be crossed to obtain a winning number. This party line crossover in search of votes will be most fruitful in the high vote potential precincts already identified. This is because the socio-economic factors of "middle-class neighborhoods" will have manifested themselves in the vote of the precinct, regardless of the nominal registration.

Non-Partisan Races

A vote analysis of a district for a non-partisan race should be done the same way as the partisan race. The vote profile of the parties, in a two party area, will give good reflections of its "conservative" tendencies.

In a non-partisan race, however, there is no such thing as a base vote (unless some "endorsing" organization can lend votes to a candidate of its choice). However, the need to know a vote target still holds. While a non-partisan candidate does not have what can be called the "luxury" of a base-vote, it can be a boon in the sense that no votes will be taken for granted.

Yet, in a non-partisan race, the contest is usually going to be decided by a relatively small number of votes. For example, a city council race could be one type of such a race, where three thousand votes will elect a candidate. There are significant advantages to such a race. The possibilities for strong personal organization are heightened. Campaign workers can see the difference one vote will make and will be more enthusiastic in the search for votes. (The same *can* be made to work in a large vote congressional race. See the Kasten Plan.[38]) The search for absentee ballot voters and a get-out-the vote organization can almost visibly count up the votes for winning. Collecting endorsing cards from potential voters can be a highly effective and motivating way for a campaign to press forward. This is so long as the campaign does not get lulled into believing that 3,000 endorsement cards will automatically translate into three thousand people who will go to the polls. If the endorsement cards were tied to a fool proof absentee ballot campaign, there might be more reason for "believing."

The Liberal's Dirty Little Secret

In the course of doing a vote analysis of the district by precincts, a strange phenomenon will often rear its ugly head, across the U.S.A. This is the "ninety percent plus" precinct. Such precincts invariably go for "liberal" candidates. To be sure, there are occasionally very small precincts which can reflect a 90% pattern once a while, but only under extremely rare occurrences.

A "usual" "ninety percent plus" precinct comes from the lower socio-economic level, usually designated an "ethnic" precinct. These precincts are "controlled." The control is usually through one or two ways, or both. First, the voters are "told" who to vote for. In this case the controlling mechanism is most often an organization which communicates its desires to the voters in a "voter slate," which is mailed out.

Such an organization (or individuals who bring about the same result) usually receives "expense" money for its troubles to do the mailer, or have precinct walkers making the contacts. Liberal candidates (usually incumbents) take care of this.

An unusual article hit a newspaper in 1976. A couple of black ministers in the slums of Oakland, California, were complaining that they had not received sufficient "walk-around" money for the election. They stated that they didn't care about the elections. What they meant was, without "walk-around money," there would be no vote delivery.[39] Obviously, this sort of thing rarely hits the newspapers.

The other way that the controlled precincts are worked, is through the vote mechanism. The "found" votes are added to the ledger, usually in the polling place, after the polls close. Quite often some attempt is made to cover over the added votes by adding signatures to the sign-in ledger, which the voters use. From time to time allegations are made in the press that an investigation showed "several" sign-in signatures appeared to be from the same person. Rarely does anything happen from such investigations.

Another widely used method is an absentee ballot from a county hospital. Ballots can be passed around for signatures and then voted as the controlling persons see fit. Many times the ballots are not even passed out, instead, there is a ballot signing "party."

When one party is sufficiently ensconced in an area, absentee ballots even get "lost." Because more Republicans avail themselves of absentee ballots, often an address gives a solid clue as to the vote inside. In the past, a major change in the number of absentee ballots cast was a clue that something might have been "funny." However, with the advent over the past several election cycles of more people using absentee ballots, a "bulge" in absentee ballots is losing the attention getting profile it once had.

In the course of the discussion on swing vote precincts, it was seen how important marginal votes are. Swing voters are often the ones who make or break an election. Therefore, if "controlled" precincts could have their fraudulent vote decreased by heightened scrutiny, a challenger could reap the reward.

If a campaign could afford the manpower, at least one or two people should be assigned to study the mechanics of the district's vote distribution, collection, and tabulation mechanisms. An in-depth understanding of the pressure points would lead to avenues in which to threaten, or pressure, a controlled vote. As pointed out here, the sign-in book with names and addresses of the voters can be a key instrument. With computerized tabulation of voting machines totals, the sign-in book can be an important indicator at the source of the problem.

Obviously, the best way to police the precincts would be to have the voting judge position of the party filled in the precinct. However, quite often in the precincts, which are obviously abusing vote totals, there is a great reluctance on the part of poll watchers to go to these precincts. In Harris county, Texas, (Houston), the forms, which precinct poll watchers used in order to volunteer for duty (in the '70's), had a category called "hostile" precincts. It was often hard enough to get poll watchers to cover most of the precincts, let alone all of them and especially in the "controlled" areas.

The problem is hard to attack, but is worthy of attention. Certainly, a public attack on it in most cases is not possible. The pious liberal "how could you" of the opposition would be deafening along with shouts of racism, elitism, and "gutter politics." (This is, of course, if a public accusation were acknowledged by the opposition party or the local media—instead of just being ignored.) Also, a charge of potential vote fraud would be made to sound self-serving and would tag the candidate or campaign as "shrill."

The least that should be done is to make the problem of "problem" precincts known to the opposition. This could take the form of several discussions, not just one or two, with the county elections clerk on the subject. In any county, except the improbable one which has the electoral machinery controlled strictly by friendly forces to your campaign, such an inordinate interest in the elections machinery would get communicated to the enemy camp. Wishful thinking would have it that the "other side" would "tone down" the public vote fraud, which would hold it down somewhat.

Topics for discussion with the county clerk could be along the lines of how obvious the bias is in the vote totals of some precincts. Or, questions could be asked about how absentee ballots are handled in the county hospital. And, further, how could "interested citizens" verify that the ballots were in fact used by the people who sent them. Another subject could be how voting machines are distributed, as compared with the break down by area party registration or some other formula. [If suburban voting takes place before normal work hours, and, then after work hours, the distribution of voting machines can be important. Distribution could either alleviate or exacerbate the lines people stand-in to vote, which could have an effect on vote totals.]

Feeding a story to a friendly person in the media as an item of interest could be useful. If the opposition knows that quite a bit of interest has been paid to the election mechanics, and then a story hits the media, the opposition will know where it is coming from. That is in fact the whole idea. Shine a light, even if not much else can be done. It will make the controllers a little more cautious and this might save some votes.

One possible avenue for action would be to have a "flying squad" to go into some of the bad precincts just before the polls close to see what the count of voters has been in the sign-in book and to get a glance at a page of signatures. By knowing the number of those signed in, the total vote should not change after the polls have closed. However, the election law of the state in question must be known explicitly as to rights of "public inspection." Such immediate inspection would have a chilling effect on post-closing "found" votes. This could, however, get bad publicity for the initiator of the "flying squad."

The trade off for a campaign, which would consider such tactics, is the chilling effect of getting people to go to inner city polling places after dark. The question of the efficient expenditure of resources comes to the fore. Could the same resources ("flying squads") be better used to get out the vote in friendly territory?

In 1996, the county Republican party in Orange County, California, hired uniformed "observers" to go to the polls. The goal was to keep illegal immigrant, non-citizens, from voting. In the 46th Congressional District that year, where "B-1" Bob Dornan lost his congressional seat to Democrat Loretta Sanchez, subsequent investigations showed considerable vote fraud by illegal Mexican immigrants voting. Yet in spite of the "facts," and even taking the evidence to the U.S. House of Representatives (controlled by the Republicans), they could not find enough "courage" to overturn the results. The braying of the Democrats about voter "intimidation" after that action by the Republicans was still being heard in the mid-'90's. The din and hue and cry the Democrats sent up was about how the awful Republicans were trying to intimidate legitimate Hispanic voters from exercising their right to vote. [It shouldn't be too hard to guess in which direction the liberal media turned its hand wringing and finger pointing.]

In this day and age of closer and closer elections, the problem of vote "control" must be looked after. Of course, "control" is a very strong word. However, suspicions are aroused by examples such as the following:

[While the examples given here are vote totals for U.S. Senate races, the same proportion of the reported lopsided totals was actually seen in all races in these precincts in the particular election.] In 1972 in North Carolina, Jesse Helms, the Republican, ran against Nick Galifianakis, a Democrat. In Greensboro precinct number 5, Helms, who won the state wide race, won a total of 9 votes (nine) versus 734 for Galifianakis. That is 1.2% of the vote for Helms. Greensboro precinct 6 gave Helms 18 votes and 810 to Galifianakis. In Greensboro number 7, Helms got 20 votes versus 727 for Galifianakis.

On the other side of the country, consider the 1976 U.S. Senate race between John Tunney, Democrat, and S.I. Hayakawa, Republican. Hayakawa won the race, but look at some interesting results from Oakland, California. In precinct 42020, Hayakawa got 13 votes compared to Tunney's 222. Precinct 42060 went 19 for Hayakawa and 211 against him. Hayakawa got ten votes in precinct 42170 compared to Tunney's 266.

Anyone seriously watching or studying the 1960 presidential race knows that Nixon lost the race in Illinois, and that massive fraud was alleged. However, unfortunately, few people are aware how close to home the problem really is.

Many liberals, like the Teddy Kennedys of this world, have a nasty little secret going for them. Their pious pronouncements and platitudes about "participatory democracy" pale in the light of understanding how many and how such politicians actually get into office.

The "real-politik" of the problem is that even if the problems of a controlled vote were to be convincingly documented, the question is, then what? What campaign has the resources to fight the battle *after* the election and in the courts? Then again, what may be "documented" and what happens in a courtroom can be two different things. The L.A.P.D. thought it had "documented" evidence, DNA evidence, and a time line to show that O.J. Simpson had committed two murders. The court jury had other thoughts.

Get Out the Vote

A prioritization of precincts according to a potential vote will also give a campaign priority precincts for getting out the vote on election day. The greater the potential for swing votes, the greater the potential for an impact on the voters on election day.

It has been this writer's experience, from sitting on many telephone banks in order to get out the vote on election day, that phoning into areas where the solid base vote is likely to come from, is not productive. The people who form the base of a conservative's vote are already conscientious about exercising their franchise. Therefore, "persuadable" voters should be focused upon for an election day push.

It would greatly benefit a campaign to be able to assign one person for planning the "get out-the-vote" drive. This person would organize and plan for the final day through out the campaign. He/she would take into account the resources that were available during the campaign and factor them into some other resources, which may be available only on election day, such as "one day volunteers."

The best method for the "get out the-vote" drive is, of course, the telephone. Because of the impracticality of setting up anything like a phone bank for just one day (because of costs, at least for most campaigns) the job will have to be done by home phones. There is a prejudice against using home phones on the part of most professionals, however, because it is so hard to exercise any control. However, the urgency, immediacy, and understanding of the participants on the one day, election day, should largely overcome this objection by the pro's.

Precinct lists with telephone numbers must be distributed to the volunteers. The targeted voters will then be called. While it is nice to have sufficient numbers of people to make the calls between 5:00 PM and 7:00 PM, which leaves an hour before the polls close, the numbers involved to do such a large job are impractical. The logistics of a massive home phoning program can be understood by dividing the number of targeted voters by the number of calls that can be made by one volunteer. Even dedicated volunteers are going to fade in enthusiasm after spending about two hours on the telephone. Just getting the volunteers to distribute the precinct lists is a massive job, which will take considerable time in planning.

For a thoroughly rigorous and detailed approach to a "get out the vote" program, see the Kasten Plan, note 38 in the section of notes. What the Kasten Plan outlines is a program with vote totals as goals for each precinct, get-out-the-vote teams, and election night "parties," which focus on getting assigned voters out, etc.

7

Organizing

A campaign organization is no different from any other organization. It must have certain goals toward which it is working, and it needs a reason for belonging on the part of its members.

A campaign organization will usually come to life based upon some "willing volunteers" who know the candidate. The degree to which the candidate understands what should happen in a campaign is the degree to which the organization will develop at the beginning. One West Coast congressional candidate hired a campaign manager and told him, "You do whatever you're supposed to do with an organization. I'll take care of the campaigning."

In the crush of a candidate's filing for office and having some nomination activities taken care of, an organization can start off completely amorphous and with little apparent direction. It will succeed to the degree that it understands the following needs.

1. There must be an endorsing level for the organization. This is a group of prominent people in the community who will put their name to the use of the campaign.
2. There must be a strategy level of the campaign, which decides how the campaign will get and direct its resources.

3. There must be a working level of the campaign which carries out the tactics necessary for realizing the strategy.

For campaigns not being run by professional consultants, until a basic district inventory is made, no coherent grand strategy can be worked out. The results of the inventorying process will usually not be ready for the beginning of a campaign, but rudiments of the district inventory need to be available for early decisions. The candidate and two or three friends will be best advised to do the preliminary work themselves. Searching out influence centers can start at any time from the beginning of the development of an inventory, but the basic organizational work needs a direction/framework laid out for it. The candidate must give that direction. A candidate who leaves it all up to a campaign manager at the beginning, should a person be filling such a slot, will have lost direction from the beginning.

Kitchen Cabinet

A "kitchen cabinet" needs to be formed with three or four people, or so, whose judgment the candidate respects. This group will set the grand strategy of the campaign. Persons to avoid for this group are "cognoscente" or campaign "know-it-alls." Know-it-alls are the most "media influenced" and will bog the meetings down in "issues" talk. Arguing orthodoxy or philosophical stands is not the duty of the kitchen cabinet. This group must make the hard decisions of whose support to go after and in which areas resources will be used.

The group must be kept small, because of the multiplicity of subjects, which will be covered. This will effectively preclude getting opinions from too many people sitting around a table. The group must be small, also, to be comfortable with itself. Personality conflicts or empire building are minimized when a small number of people have a constant interchange of ideas. Also, the group must be small and dedicated to be able to meet regularly with little absenteeism. Should someone leave the campaign, their replacement must be brought up to date with the same information that the others have. Again, too many people cannot fill such positions.

The kitchen cabinet will start the work of searching out the endorsing committee of the candidate. Any campaign, which expects to be taken seriously by the community, must have a representative committee of community opinion leaders listed as the basis of the campaign. These people let the community know that the campaign is "real." When the candidate is asked, "who is supporting you?" this is the group of people the candidate will refer to. Again, the basic district inventory will indicate areas from which these leaders may come. Necessity dictates that most of the "endorsers" will be known by the candidate and the kitchen cabinet, already. However, it is a matter of choosing and asking the people. Too many campaigns are unaware of the importance which other community opinion leaders place on the community status of the chairman(person) of the campaign. Some campaigns, to get around the problems of the beginning stage of a campaign, will establish two or three co-chairs so that later in the campaign other names may be added.

Research Committee

The next step in organizing is to set up a research committee, which will begin the in-depth work of the district inventory and the vote inventory. Two or three people, who are willing to put in the time and effort in order to fully collect and study the material, are best. This is as compared to a large group, which can become unwieldy and descend into interminable debates about "issues."

A campaign, which gets to this level of organization, will have taken a quantum leap, compared to other campaigns. The kitchen cabinet will be seeking more people for the endorsement committee.

Endorsers will be told that no meetings will be necessary, that they are the letterhead committee of the organization. However, the campaign should be clear that the endorser should be willing to make a phone-call introduction, or so, for the candidate in order to meet more influential people. The endorser group can start sponsored lunches with the candidate and other influential people, also. In addition, at a later date, endorsers will be asked to send out some notes of support.

During this time, the research committee has been gathering and sorting out information on inventories. By this time, basic secretarial help will be a necessity as lunches and courting of influential people gets underway. Also, a person who will do basic coordination of the campaign's efforts will be necessary.

Courting

The process of courting influential people must hit an early stride and continue throughout the campaign to the degree that the candidate has time. Even a school board race, which may be decided by only three thousand votes cast, will discover in its inventorying efforts, that there are many more influential people "out there" than the candidate could possibly meet. This is a main function of the kitchen cabinet to decide whom to seek out.

Another function of the kitchen cabinet is to decide what course of concentration the campaign will take for the fall run. From Labor Day until the first Tuesday after the first Monday in November, is only about eight weeks. All steps for the campaign push will have had to be mapped out. The campaign push, of course, is the people-intensive part of the campaign, whether this is precinct organizing, signs posting, telephone boiler rooms, "dear friend" cards, or whatever. The campaign will have had to map out the intensive recruiting drive that will lead to the accomplishment of the final push.

Many campaigns get entirely too ambitious. They set up a multitude of projects to be accomplished, which all too often are only partially done.

Too many fits and starts can demoralize campaign workers with a "what's the use" attitude, even if they stay with the campaign. What comes out of the efforts is a distraction, rather than a contribution, to the feeling of accomplishment which a campaign needs and tries to communicate to the public.

Overly Ambitious

An example of being overly ambitious has been conjured up as an example by some campaign workers. They envisioned a campaign in a mid-west congressional district listing no fewer than thirteen major projects as "priority" measures to get done in about three months. The workers also projected what the likely outcome would be—internally for the campaign that attempted such a route. The plan was:

1. A major "letters to the editor" campaign for the significant newspapers in the district. 2. A "camper caravan" to work shopping centers for a least four weekends. 3. A major absentee ballot drive designed to increase the vote turnout. 4. A fully organized bumper sticker campaign with squads of people asking people to put the stickers on (right there, in the parking lots). 5. A literature distribution squad for passing campaign materials out to the women waiting in their cars (nothing else to read . . .) for their children after school. 6. Another literature distribution squad for passing out materials to lines of people waiting to go into the movies. 7. A tennis tournament in the name of the candidate, complete with major donated prizes from local businesses. 8. A "mobile banner" squad with large "Vote for Smith" banners, for holding up at key overpasses and intersections during rush-hours. 9. A brass band for playing at shopping centers on a regular basis. 10. A "fertilizer squad" to spread fertilizer on key hillocks around the district, which would sufficiently darken the grass

that "Vote for Smith" would become a living sign. 11. An "operation I.D." program to pass out engravers for people to identify their household goods with their driver's license number to discourage crime. In this one, generous campaign propaganda was to be included with the engraving tool as to how the candidate was doing more than talking about crime . . . 12. A handicapped person telephone brigade to make recruiting calls for volunteers from their homes. 13. A major volunteer lawn sign program designed to get out 2,000 signs on residential lawns.

The list of events was designed to be a supplement to an ambitious "dear friend" postcard campaign, priority precinct organizing for walking, and a telephone boiler room operation.

The result of such a program would be demoralization of a campaign. At each steering committee meeting, the campaign manager would read off the list of projects, like a litany, for "reports" on the part of the people who were in charge of the projects. As the weeks would pass, one after another of the projects would be scaled back, retrenched, and finally, eliminated. The meetings would become a spectacle for the participants to see what the excuses would be on the part of the project "directors," as to why they had not made more progress. Also, there would be excuses on the part of the campaign manager, as to why more money and resources could not be offered to help the projects that were still limping forward.

The same campaign would have made its fundraising drive just another project—inserted into the "master list." The man in charge would be prominent in the community, but his "commission" would be "to get some money for the campaign." This man also would squirm at steering committee meetings, when his turn would come to make a report on fundraising progress. He would feel the enmity of the group, as he too would make excuses for the lack of funds coming in. The result of no money would be obvious: it would prevent the purchase of much literature for the one project which was relatively healthy: the afternoon school auto line-up literature distribution.

The fund raising chair would not submit himself to such flagellation after the second meeting. He would become "too busy" to attend further meetings.

By the end of September, the campaign would be seeing volunteers melting away, at the very time the reverse should have been happening. Not only would the recruits leave the campaign, but the word would spread widely that the campaign was a fast sinking ship. This would spread to "would-be" contributors, which would cause the second man appointed as fundraising chair to quit.

Such a hypothetical horror story would not have to happen to a campaign, if it were organized under the guidelines set forth in *Campaigning To Win*.

Only a couple of the many projects from the "cafeteria style" of campaign would have been needed to form the core or "events background" of a winning campaign. This assumes that they would have been intelligently organized and executed.

Clearly, the whole program would have been much too ambitious. It would have required hundreds of highly motivated and dedicated volunteers willing to put in hundreds of hours of time. The organizational talents necessary to coordinate all the events would have boggled the minds of the best Jaycees.

So much for hypothetical campaigns focusing on overly ambitious project development.

Precinct Lists

From the basic campaign organization set forth here, the first major undertaking requiring a sizable number of people is the rationalization of precinct lists. This is nothing more than organizing the lists and putting telephone numbers against the names and addresses so that the lists may be used by campaign workers. The form that precinct lists take will dictate the amount of work that must be put into them. However, in all cases, the campaign must have the names, addresses and telephone numbers of potential voters in a usable form, which can readily be moved from one volunteer to another.

The lists will be used for postcard addressing and recruiting more postcard writers.

Vote Accumulation Drive

Based upon the type of district, the kitchen cabinet must decide whether to base its vote accumulation drive on the mails, telephoning, candidate walking, or some mix. With an eye on the financial requirements of the means employed to impact the voters, the vote goal of the campaign is the obvious target. Whether the race is congressional or school board, the voters must still be contacted several times *to be asked for their vote*. A campaign must be able to implement a drive that touches on each necessary vote. This is the real "stuff" of a campaign. Candidate appearances, newsreleases, and position papers aside, the basic campaign is the rote contact of voters.

A campaign, 1. which contacts each targeted voter, individually, several times to ask for the vote, 2. which is visible to the voters by means of some sort of signs, and 3. which is "validated" through opinion makers in the community, is going to be in extremely good shape for election day.

This does not mean that a phone call or a sign will accomplish the task. A campaign must establish its presence. This means an identity in the mind of the voter. A mailer, which many parties send out on behalf of the party ticket does very little to identify a specific campaign, once the voter looks at the picture of the nominee for governor and senator. A candidate for congress or the state legislature gets lost in the shuffle in "party precinct literature drops," when five different pieces of campaign literature are left at each target home in a precinct.

The Way to Do It

Three distinct contacts with the voter should be a basic campaign goal. Postcards are best. Campaign workers will need to be recruited to write the postcards, right from the precinct lists. Often, campaign volunteers from the party or personal friends of the candidate can start the writing, but later, volunteer recruiting will need to be done.

The postcards should be written preferably by someone geographically close to the recipients: The undated postcards should be collected for mailing on a given, targeted date. The message is very simple: "I'm writing because I think Joe White should represent us in Congress. Please consider voting for him. Sincerely, Mary Trout, Pinetree Drive."

The second contact is similar. "We need Joe White in Congress. Please vote for him. Sincerely, Jill Conrad, Saltmarsh Avenue." The third postcard need only say, "Please vote for Joe White for Congress. He needs your vote this Tuesday. Sincerely, Jean Swallow, Watershed Road."

A household, which receives three postcards from the campaign, must be impressed with the effort. Furthermore, the voters receiving the cards and seeing the candidate's signs around the district will be impressed because of the reinforcement of the appearance of action. The knockout punch comes from hearing someone who is respected in the community say that Joe White is someone to vote for.

Ecology and environment freaks notwithstanding, campaign signs are a necessity. A district's voters must be made aware that a public side to the campaign exists. Bumper stickers can qualify as presenting a public side of the campaign, but they must be diligently pressed into service. A virtual campaign must be made of getting the strips *onto* car bumpers, *not* just into the hands of potential users. Or, even a day glow symbol of some sort, readily perceived, in one corner of auto windows, can get around some problems with bumper strips. For instance, a bright red day-glow ball four inches in diameter would grab attention, once sufficient numbers were dispensed and circulated in a district. The curiosity aroused on the part of the people seeing so many cars with the bright red day glow ball in the lower left rear auto window would cause a stir. This would more than compensate for not having the name of the candidate more readily legible.

The only efficacy of any such device or gimmick (in lieu of signs) is in mass posting (in cars or however) throughout the district. The necessity for mass distribution holds for lawn signs, also. A persevering effort must be made for getting the signs out, if they are to be used in the campaign. Or, sniping signs, which are posted on existing sign posts or on their own framework, are effective. Sniping signs are of many sizes, quite often 14" by 40." The job they fill is to spread the candidate's name throughout the district. See the page of sign examples.

The task of erecting sniper signs or lawn signs is a large one (if not done by a paid professional). A professional political sign posting company figures about 1,500 sniper signs will just adequately cover an average California Assembly seat district (this is roughly half the size of a U.S. Congressional seat's geographical area). Similar coverage for a congressional district, then, would be about 3,000 signs. Political districts of other sizes can be compared to how their area relates to that of a congressional district. The variables of rural, suburban, and urban campaigns are infinite. However, 3,000 signs to impact 400,000 people in a congressional district do not "paper" the district.

Considerable time must go into a sign effort to make it work. Volunteer recruitment, location recruitment for homes, and follow up during the campaign, as signs are torn down, is necessary.

The problem of people complaining about signs cluttering up the district should be approached on a numbers basis. Many people will see the signs who otherwise would have been unaware of the campaign. This has got to be worth the risk of an occasional sneer about "visual pollution." If the other parts of the campaign are worked as set forth here, the campaign will be perceived as a hard working campaign, which will get admiration for plain hard work. The sneers about pollution will come from the opposition, worried about the impact of a solidly executed campaign. See the section, here, about pressure on the candidate.

Precinct Walking

Many activists have heard of candidates who won based upon rigorous precinct walking. Many other candidates have tried walking and have been disappointed in the results. Merely walking a precinct will not produce measurable results. It must be done right. As with the rest of the basic campaign outlined here, the goal of all activities is mutual reinforcement. The same holds even for walking.

Walk up to a person's door, and they will wonder what you want. Tell them your name, and it will be forgotten before you leave the porch. Hand them a brochure, and it will be put down and forgotten because the person was doing something before the door bell rang. These are the problems to overcome.

A lead person who rings the doorbell first and announces that "Jones the candidate is on his way" breaks the ice and is the back drop for Jones to mention his name again. The lead person also saves the candidate from waiting at an empty house. Jones can give a brochure and a "people card" (see the chapter on media, here). A stringer volunteer walking with Jones can be carrying the precinct list for Jones to greet the people by name. Also, the stringer can mark down positive reactions of the people for later postcards, or other types of recruiting for help.

[As the use of computers and electronic mail spreads, and depending on the demographics involved in a given district, ask for an e-mail address. The request would be while talking with the person at the house. The stated reason, "to keep you posted on the campaign, if you're interested," could be a powerful way to build an interest group to support the candidate. While not necessarily organized as such, it becomes an ad hoc "e-mailers for Jones" affinity group, with some obvious uses for the campaign.]

Furthermore, a stringer can carry bulk brochures for Jones so that the candidate stays looking cool, instead of like a person burdened down with literature.

After the walking has been done, another postcard [e-mail follow-up] is a must. The reinforcement of the postcard saying, "it was nice meeting you" makes all the difference. This cements the candidate in the mind of the voter. On top of the other postcards, strong reinforcement has taken place. This can take the place of one of the postcard mailings, previously covered.

In short, basic human contact will win votes. A basic campaign, as outlined here, needs to be done with no short cuts. (Pre-printed postcards will not do. Everyone is curious about a handwritten postcard addressed to them. They will read the message side, if handwritten. Printed words start to lose people as soon as the people see that the card is not personal. There are too many commercial applications of preprinted postcards.)

Three Pronged Attack

Therefore, a three pronged attack of postcards, signs, and personal influence is a rock solid base and will be a major undertaking to accomplish properly. The beauty of such an approach is that it is simple and all other campaign activities may be imposed upon such a foundation. However, subtract any of these basics and even a slick media campaign will not cover the "reach" possible from a basic contact campaign, properly done. An apparent glaring omission from such a basic campaign is that no provision has been made, yet, for candidate public appearances, position statements, or general "campaigning." All of these efforts come after the basics outlined above.

After seeking the support of influential people, after recruiting volunteers for postcards, after pouring over maps for the placing of signs, then, the campaign can write newsreleases and speeches. However, the critical trade-off of most-impact-for-the-time-and-money must be weighed.

Even one "wine and cheese" tasting for fundraising purposes can use up a couple of weeks of work by several people for armtwisting in ticket sales, planning and coordinating. This compares to the fact that one person can write about 500 postcards (with the first message outlined above) in four nights of 2–1/2 hours per night. Two such people could contact 1,000 voters in the time it would take to plan and find 100 people to go to a wine taster. Further, the 100 people at the wine-taster would most likely be already inclined to vote for the candidate. On top of this, fund raising is more efficient in other ways.

Or, consider the tired and hackneyed trap of organizing campaign "coffees." For the hours expended in putting the coffees or teas together and cajoling people into cajoling others to attend such an event, many, many voters could otherwise be contacted. In the crush of a campaign year, few candidates realize how few people know what congressional [or school, or hospital] district they live in. Even fewer candidates will realize how long the average person will remember the name of the candidate he/she has just met, or what the campaign is for.

A final word on the "basic" campaign. During the course of a campaign, candidates and campaign workers will focus upon the signs they are putting out, ask about letters they have sent out, or search out items in the newspaper regarding the campaign. But, the average voter is not searching out such information, and in fact, is missing most of it. Campaigns at levels below those spotlighted in the media, over the course of the whole campaign, will be able to count the total exposure of the campaign to the "average voter" in only seconds. That is, through the life of the campaign, even for a well financed congressional race, the average voter will have seen or focused upon the news of the race or the campaign propaganda a total of a few minutes at most.

There are just too many distractions in the mail, the airwaves and street signs for everyone else. With "selective perception," most people tune out political materials such as bulk mail, 30 second spots, and appeals to attend political rallies. They are plain not interested. This "shield" can be penetrated with vast media and mailing expenditures, or a personalized approach. The basic campaign approach, here, asks the voter for a vote. Ask enough people, personally, often enough, and the votes will be there. The lowly postcard meets these requirements, when used in conjunction with the other approaches described.

Boiler Rooms

Some comments on boiler room phone operations are in order. The bias of the author is against boiler room operations, per se. However, many political professionals speak highly of such operations and can reference highly successful campaigns.

A classic boiler room is filled with telephones and staffed with enough people to keep the phones going eight or ten hours per day. May Ellen Miller's "Boiler Room Operation" is the bible of the approach, printed by the National Republican Congressional Committee, 1974. As she says in her preface: "The design of any telephone operation must be made with the thought in mind of adequate financing, volunteers available to do the job and a determination that it must go with precision. The key ingredients to a successful telephone operation are training and supervision. It is also absolutely essential to give assiduous attention to details of each part of the program . . ."

The expenses involved in phone deposits and calling charges are one negative to such a program. Various telephone companies throughout the country have been burned too many times by past campaigns. Cash up front is the rule now. Another problem with phone banks is the difficulty of recruiting volunteers. This is especially so when comparing the willingness of people to write postcards versus working a telephone. A third problem with phone banks is that they are "real time." The recipient is disturbed at that moment for the call. None of these problems are encountered when using postcards. Lastly, the phone operation is not usually considered to a "campaigning tool."

A boiler room operation is usually considered to be an identification tool for use in a get-out-the-vote operation. The boiler room identifies favorably inclined voters to the candidate during the campaign. Then, the favorable potential voters are recontacted on, or immediately before, election day to get their vote out . For most candidates who begin with low name recognition/identification, this type of operation is not realistic. On the other hand, to actually make three contacts by telephone to ask for a voter's vote would come across as silly.

In Sum

An election campaign is formed to seek out votes. If that campaign touches opinion leaders and voters both privately and publicly in asking for votes, the basic job is being done. An efficient campaign goes about these tasks as simply and straight forward as possible. This is the most efficient way.

The candidate and the kitchen cabinet are the brains of the campaign. A research committee finds required information for inventories. Volunteers sow materials and signs throughout the district. A basic campaign will thus reach voters, place signs, mail postcards and make private contact with influential people.

8

Salesmanship

In their zeal to discuss issues, far too many candidates can be counted upon to urge cliche types of actions, such as "balance the budget!" Yet few ever ask the question of this issue (or other cliche types of issues), "By stating that we must balance the budget, how many campaign workers will turn out, how many dollars will be contributed, or how many votes will come as a direct result of the statement?"

There is an almost fatal idealism involved in making "political statements." The idealism is that the statements will be translated in the mind of the listener into a call for action. It does not happen that way. A listener does not hear the statement, "the budget must be balanced" and translate it into the meaning that, if he (the listener) will walk precincts to get votes to elect Jones, that Jones will get the budget balanced, which will stop inflation, create new jobs and raise the standard of living, so that the listener can buy that red sports car he has always wanted. To repeat, it doesn't work that way.

Votes are won only by actions. Somebody, somewhere, somehow must take the actions that will get votes. These actions can only come through the campaign workers, the campaign donors, and the voters themselves. If a particular statement does not motivate people to work for a campaign, or motivate them to donate money to a campaign, or to vote, what good is the statement? Because time is limited, any action on the part of a candidate or campaign, which does not produce people, money, or votes is actually losing all of these! The loss of time means the loss of the ability to use that time to get more resources.

In the fullest sense of the word, a campaign must exercise salesmanship. "Salesmanship" is motivating someone to take an action. The motivation needs to come about through stimulating people's self interest.

Campaigns need to consider all contacts with people as prospective sales opportunities. While the "masses" are "prospects" for help with the campaign, people in most cases must be asked for their help, individually. Further, they need to be given a reason to give up something else to give their help.

During the campaign season, all over the country campaigns will be holding teas and coffees to "meet the candidate." In these meetings a candidate usually holds forth on different issues and toward the end of the talk he/she, or a worker, will state that the campaign needs help. However, the statement is expected to be made and the group takes it as a pro forma statement, because "that's what campaigns do." It is a rare campaign which uses the time to talk about the joys of meeting the constituents of the district, or about how the campaign organization is going to post signs all over the district, and, "who here can let us put a sign in their front yard?"

It is a rare candidate in the context of the tea or coffee who asks the ladies in attendance for *their* solution to Medicaid or Medicare. The candidate who has some questions designed with three choices to offer the listener can get that person's ideas on a question. This can be followed up with, "why?" Long-winded replies can be cut short with a comment along the lines of, "I appreciate your views, but I should ask some more people for their views to get to know how the group is thinking. You've got some good ideas on that. Would you be willing to let us put a sign up in your front yard? (Or, to address postcards, etc.,) By definition, people who attend such political functions are making a commitment to action (even if they had their arms twisted mercilessly to attend the event). Get the action.

Good salesmanship is letting the other person talk. Just as the sweetest words in the language to a given person are his or her own name, so too are his or her opinions. The act of listening to another person's opinions is an indication of interest in the person. Accordingly, people will be interested in people who are interested in them.

A candidate who holds forth on his/her erudition on issues across the spectrum is exercising no salesmanship. Stating fifteen reasons why the country needs the B-2 Stealth Bomber is not, in-and-of itself, going to convince people to give up one or two evenings per week to help the campaign (unless the listeners are employees of Northrop Grumman in Pico Rivera or Hawthorne, California, where the planes are made. THAT would be a *real* "issue" in those cities). After the election, the winner can talk, as long as people will listen, on the "issues," but before the election, there is only time to ask for help and keep getting more votes.

Of course, campaigns are made up of more than political gatherings, where people can be considered to be interested in politics. However, along the lines of the chapter here on people's basic interests guiding them into one activity or another, an assumption is that most people have put politics low in their hierarchy of interests. In such a case, asking for their vote is a positive expression of interest in them by the candidate.

Fundraising

The area of fundraising is rife with the error of not seeking out the prospective donor's interests. A person is inclined to support his or her own interests to the degree that they can, and this will be in proportion to the level of passion focused on those interests. Most campaigns do not know whether funds, which are donated, represent an investment in the campaign or a "buy-off" to get out from under the pressure of being solicited. An investment based on "interests" will usually be many times the size of the minimum level necessary to buy out or "buy-off."

Any campaign would be well advised to heed what Stan Holden quoted supersalesman John Handick as saying. In an article, "Everybody Sells Something," Handick said, " . . . everybody sells something. Every person is constantly trying to sell his ideas . . . his opinions . . . his own point of view . . . his own special interests."[40]

If a voter could believe that a candidate's interests significantly paralleled those of the voter, and that the candidate is likely to get into a position to be able to do something about their mutual interests, then the voter is potentially likely to make a very large investment in time and money to support that candidate.

9

Issues

The great bottomless grab-bag of "issues" is most often a black hole of wasted time for political campaigns. Every campaign precinct walker knows just what "issues" would win a race. Any local barber or beautician can instantly recommend just "the" issue for any level of campaign—an issue so powerful it would propel a local candidate instantly into any office he or she wanted. It would be also an issue so strong it would toss any incumbent headlong out of office. Anyone who doubts this need only ask that barber, stylist or beautician. The leitmotif of all the various "experts" which a candidate encounters in his or her own campaign and on the campaign trail has to do with "the winning issue." It can come in different forms, but usually it is couched along the lines of "all ya gotta do is . . . ," or, "if the voters only knew."

Conservative Sameness

Yet, in spite of so many "experts," the paradox of conservative campaigns is that they usually come out sounding the same. "'I seek election to the Congress because the philosophic and political differences between Smith and myself are clear cut and I can represent all the people of the 8th Congressional District better than he, Jones said in announcing he would seek the GOP nomination."[41]

A newspaper ad finishes its copy in a political advertisement: "Norm wants to hear your concerns and to let you know about him and his campaign to restore a balanced budget and an end to deficit spending."[42]

As it was shown in the chapter on "political misinformation," the problem of what an issue is, or is not, is extremely blurred. A well-intentioned campaign will start out with "good ideas" and in the crunch of the reality of the time and resources at its disposal, falls into the hackneyed standard fair that has become so familiar. **Standard campaign rhetoric fails because it confuses advocacy with education all the while never understanding that in fact the task of the campaign is neither.** Education purports to make known what is not known. Advocacy purports to plead or advocate.

The following is from a U.S. Senate campaign brochure, but it is very familiar to those who practice the arcane and mildly masochistic sport of actually reading the copy of political brochures from political campaigns. The copy speaks of the need for a second revolution in America, "a revolution against the needless regulation of their lives by their own government; a revolution against mindless programs which produce more unkept promises; a revolution against the growing power of special interests who are more committed to preserving their favored past than in pioneering for our future . . . I cannot in good conscience turn my back on the challenge which our state and our nation now face. We need desperately to believe once more in ourselves, our country, and our future."[43]

Not only political brochures, but political newspaper copy comes over with the same familiar ring from conservative campaigns. Most Republican candidates for Congress would recognize the following verbiage. In an article, "Conservative Goes After [Smith's] Berth," the reporter focuses on the conservative: "He calls himself 'the' anti-inflation candidate and says he hopes to capitalize, not only on [Smith's] reputation as a free spender on the campaign trial, but also on his liberal voting record in Congress. He accused [Smith] of not caring about inflation, saying, 'He only cares about cultivating his liberal image and promoting wasteful social welfare programs.'"[44]

Two years later in the same congressional district against the same liberal congressman, the next conservative challenger in line was saying, "The only government we need is government to do the things we can't do for ourselves. This translates into reduced government, lowered taxes, decreased legislation and more efficiency."[45]

The "issue" of inflation is instructive as to the handling of an issue by both sides of an issue. The conservative position is all too familiar to those who understand free enterprise economics and the problem of the large government deficits. But, that has nothing to do with the way an issue is handled in the context of a political campaign.

As has been shown, conservatives laid into inflation in 1974 and attempted to tie the blame for inflation onto the "big spenders" in the Democrat controlled Congress. However, to the consternation of the conservatives, the Democrats did not roll over and play dead.

One conservative candidate ran an advertisement in a local newspaper quoting the National Taxpayers Union to the effect that the incumbent congressman was one of the biggest spenders in Congress. In response to the paid political advertisement, the congressman made remarks to a local Rotary club luncheon. The remarks were carried in a rather long report on the speech in the same newspaper. The congressman said "that he is not one of Congress' big spenders despite his rating as such by the National Taxpayers Union, which he described as a radical organization. He said the Union had based its statement on bills selected by it, but that he knows of no way to answer the question, 'who is the biggest spender in Congress?' (He) said that when the voting records of all members of Congress on all appropriation bills are taken into consideration, 'I come out $34 billion less' than the total Congress voted to spend during the current session. I am amazed at the businessmen, who take this radical organization seriously,' he said."

The article continued on, "Actually, (he) said, the present Congress has reduced federal spending. He said that in 1972, the federal budget deficit was $25 billion, but that the current deficit was about $23 billion. Saying that current inflation is not confined to two or three countries, but is worldwide, (he) declared that 'big spending Democrats are not the cause.' Politics, he said, apparently is not related to the causes of inflation and went on to say that in 'conservative Switzerland' the inflation rate is about 12 per cent annually . . . '

The ironic clincher in the address to the Rotary Club by the congressman was when the article stated, "while President Ford's plan for fighting inflation had met with considerable criticism, (the congressman) was inclined to look on it with favor." Quoted directly, the congressman said, "I think he (President Ford) appealed to the best instincts of the American people.[46]

To the reader of the newspaper, who saw the shrill newspaper advertisements of the Republican challenger calling the congressman one of the "17 big spenders," the congressman comes across as understanding, educated, and calm in the face of a major problem (inflation). Score for the campaigns? Ten points for the congressman, none for the conservative challenger.

On the other side of the continent during the same year, 1974, and on the same issue, another incumbent Democrat congressman headed off the inflation issue. The first paragraph in an eight column inch newspaper article stated: "Inflation is the major problem facing the country today, and drastic steps must be taken if it is to be solved, according to Congressman [Brown]."[47] He proceeded to give his remedies for the "problem."

Such handling of issues as in the foregoing is a classic "set piece" confrontation, where one "army" (the opposition campaign) takes a shot at the entrenched "army" (the incumbent) or

other party. The incumbent's opposing camp then (either) fires
back, ignores the shot, or parries the thrust. In the first instance
of the congressman comparing inflation in the U.S. to that in
Switzerland, etc., he deftly turned around the issue and made
the opponent seem a little foolish for not "understanding" how
big the problem "really" was. The second instance was one of
preemption. The Congressman took the first shot, not at the opposition, but at deflecting inflation as an "issue."

What Republicans were not paying attention to, during
1974, was that the Democrats had more money, manpower,
and time to spend on avoiding the issues which the Republicans would be sure to hit. The Democratic Congressional
Campaign Committee had more staff and money than the Republican Congressional Campaign Committee that year. As
the Republicans were working up their side of the issues, the
Democrats were doing the same. The Democrats not only an-
ticipated the use of a particular issue, but they parried it,
turned it around, and could attack with it. In such set piece
battles, those who hold the ground already will most likely
continue to hold the ground.

As was mentioned in the chapter on salesmanship, here,
there was no call for action by the Republicans in their attack
on the Democrats for "causing" inflation. What so many Republican candidates failed to understand during 1974 was, that,
even if the Democrats had not responded at all to the charges
of being big spenders, there was no direct motivation based on
a particular paid political announcement for a voter to want to
vote for a challenger. Paid political announcements always say
to vote for someone. Paid political announcements always accuse the object of the ad of some sort of transgression. There is
no "news" or anything new about paid political announcements
in the area of "issues." The very same thing holds for speeches.

To reiterate, the "sameness" about conservative campaign
rhetoric comes from mixing advocacy and education in the same
communication (print, speeches, and ads). What the "battlers on

issues" fail to understand is that an "issue" must be defined before it can be argued. Yet, in political campaigns, no one sets any rules. The opposition is not going to concede anything. A conservative definition of an issue will be rejected by liberals or radicals. Also, since incumbents hold the attention of the media, and opponents do not, an "issue" will only be addressed "when," "as" and "if" the incumbent feels something can be gained from the attention gained for the incumbent, obviously.

Rush Limbaugh in his October '95 newsletter, on page 14, ran a devastating expose of how an issue was handled, when it was "convenient." Limbaugh chronicled Bill Clinton saying in 1993, what the Republicans started saying in 1995 on the subject of Medicaid and Medicare cuts. However, by the time '95 came around, it was no longer convenient for Clinton to accept the definition of the issue he had used in 1993. He was making attacks on the Republicans in '95 for saying what he said himself in '93.

The problem of time and space needs to be addressed further. The reason for the sameness of conservative rhetoric is that usually only the slogans for different "issues" can be found during the usual crunch of time during a campaign. A conservative putting a campaign together and going through the process of making a speech comes to the painful realization that he/she does not have the resources to make definitive statements on anything. A good conservative who has saved his issues of *Human Events* finds himself flipping through page after page looking for "that great article" on inflation (or any other current "issue"). Yet, once that article is found, it becomes apparent that the "focus," which the candidate needed for a particular speech (or other public remarks), is often not there.

Through the course of the campaign, as the research committee gathers materials, some haltingly good statements may be formulated. However, by that time, too much time has usually gone by, and the statements are still designed more with the "issue" in mind, than votes.

Of course, what is not addressed above is the problem of whether or not a candidate or the campaign is capable of making cogent and persuasive statements on all issues. Just because conservatives vaguely understand and agree about certain fundamentals of various issues, it does not mean those people as candidates can articulate such ideas in a public forum. The same hold true for anything on which they have no personal expertise (the campaign "expert" on economics, notwithstanding).

Business Addressing Issues

Consider some of the following discussions by businesspeople. Businesspeople are supposedly in a position to know about things like inflation. Also, as opposed to a political campaign, a top businessperson is considered to know something about what he or she is talking about. Yet, in the following, it will be seen that it is not only politicians who confuse education with advocacy.

H. Virgil Sherrill in 1975 was chairman of the Securities Industry Association. In April of that year, he delivered a speech to the Town Hall of California. The edited form of his talk was given in a long article in a business publication. The title was, "Future of the Free Enterprise System in Doubt," subtitled, "Capital crisis threatens strength of U.S. Market." The beginning of the remarks went, "Because of the pivotal part securities firms play in marshaling that essential raw material—capital—we feel a special responsibility to alert the leaders of American business to dangers that threaten our continued ability to perform this function. Unless government, the securities industry and the larger business community join in a concerted effort to confront a growing capital crisis, the U.S. capital formation mechanism . . . may be permanently crippled."

He went on to identify "the trends that threaten to permanently damage our system." There were three causes, he stated: "demand for capital is soaring; alternate sources, that is, other than equity, are shrinking; and individual participation in equity investment is sagging."

The article plodded on and on. Finally, the reader is given a prescription of sorts as to what should be done. He said, "We can, however, work to improve the depth and liquidity of securities markets and encourage greater participation by individual investors . . . We believe double taxation of dividends should be abolished . . . It seems to me that what is needed, what is in fact long overdue, is a national policy dedicated to capital sufficiency."[48]

This talk by Mr. Sherrill was given to an audience supposedly "aware" in matters economic. Yet, even that audience should have been embarrassed by the obfuscation involved in such an inarticulate presentation, which thoroughly sidestepped the problem.

However, Mr. Sherrill was not the only one to fall in to the same foggy problem. That same year, the Chase Manhattan Bank took out a full-page advertisement in the *Wall Street Journal* to warn of the same things that Mr. Sherrill had been blathering about. The Chase did little better. With a title of "Scream," the copy began, "It's time. One out of six Americans could be out of work ten years from now. 17 million unemployed idle in the streets. We're squawking. And screaming. You should be, too. Our country must change its economic direction. Now. Chase foresees a massive capital shortfall by 1985 . . ."[49]

The ad went on to give a laundry list of potential solutions. The list began, "Encourage an ever-growing base of personal savings. Establish more realistic depreciation allowances . . ." Nowhere does the ad address itself to the government as the cause of the problem in the first place. Nor does the ad explicitly say that it is in fact addressing itself to the government to do the things that are called for to alleviate the problems. [One could almost see a conservative candidate at a weekend campaign "meet the candidate coffee" exhorting the 12 ladies in attendance to "establish more realistic depreciation schedules . . ."] [Or, one might wonder if *Wall Street Journal* readers could decide which barricade to climb with their attaché case: the "more realistic depreciation allowances" barricade, or the "ever-growing base of personal savings barricade . . ."]

The above are examples of people trying to advocate something and falling flat: Almost as bad as the typical conservative candidate.

By way of ending this set of examples of people confusing education with advocacy and doing a poor job of both, consider the *Wall Street Journal* as it addressed the capital shortage problem in its editorials. The editors, were of course, trained advocates. They knew what they were doing.

The Journal addressed a series of editorials to the problem of "crowding out." In these articles they educated the reader to understand that the problem of the capital crisis was a result of the government's overwhelming deficits. They showed that the government was sucking up money from the marketplace and causing a capital shortage, inflation, high interest rates, etc. From these points they then went on to advocate. Simply and straightforwardly, the following summed up their presentation: "The only way out of this dilemma is for Congress to recognize the simple lesson that there is no free lunch. If it persists in running the kind of deficits now on the table, either it will be unleashing a new round of inflation, or it will force the economy to start eating its seed corn."[50]

The painful truth for campaigns approaching the problem of issues is that there are experts on every side of an issue. In order to present a case, education is necessary. Then, advocacy of some particular avenue of action is the next step.

A political campaign does not have the resources to attempt to make this type of effort. Not only that, but also painfully true is the fact that people do not have an attention span, interest, or inclination to subject themselves to the development, exploration, and resolution of a complex issue.

The exact same problems of handling an "issue," as seen above, are encountered in handling the Medicare issue. Campaigns will grind out lengthy newsreleases which won't be read by anyone and will be tossed out by the receiving media, but which will have taken up massive amounts of time to write.

At the risk of overkill, consider another issue from the past, that of an "energy crisis" and the way inarticulate businessmen addressed the problem. The president of a major oil company did an article in a statewide business journal. The article was called, "Why Can't We Have an Energy Policy?"[51] After some distance into the article and considerable verbiage, the author asked, "What *must* we do to help achieve a better understanding of our problems and more rational and reasonable public policy toward business and economic growth?" His answer was underwhelming. He said, "We can conduct our own affairs with the highest degree of integrity—and demand that others do the same. Finally, we must continually point out that most Americans also have a *direct* stake in the success of business." That was it! [Consider the response of the 12 ladies at that campaign coffee, when the exhortation is given: "We demand that people conduct their affairs with the highest degree of integrity. . . !]

Continuing on with the article, the author went into the question of solving the energy problem. He asked: "Why don't we call on all the talents of the private sector and government, establish realistic priorities, and start *doing* what must be done to increase America's energy self-sufficiency."

The end of the article was no less underwhelming than that seen above. "The petroleum industry has the skilled manpower, the technology and experience to help solve America's energy problems. And we're ready to help—just as I know every other part of business is prepared to aid in finding solutions for other compelling national problems. The only trouble is; so far we haven't been asked."

Undoubtedly, the President of Standard Oil of California at that time did not consider the article to be of a very high priority. The company writer who did the article was probably told to "do something on the energy crisis for that business journal." However, this was what the public saw; even if the personal remarks of the president of the company might have been considerably more trenchant in their focus on who in government was bringing about the energy crisis, and how.

The point for campaigns to understand is that they should not get into the thicket of "issues." Campaigns are made up of people who have less expertise and authority than the top businessmen quoted here. Just as these businessmen in most cases allowed an inarticulate presentation of their views, so too will a campaign have the same problem when attempting to handle "issues." This is not just for congressional campaigns. The same holds true for candidates for representative positions in state legislatures, city councils, school boards, or hospital districts.

Philip Bleiberg, a former editor of *Barron's*, in a talk given in San Francisco,[52] stated that if a person is not trained in advocacy, they shouldn't attempt it. He should have known, as a highly esteemed advocate with a national reputation. His point was that an inarticulate presentation could do more harm to the side it seeks to defend.

Manning the Barricades: A Debate

There is a tendency for conservatives to be fully convinced of the "rightness" of their positions on the "issues" of the day. This leads to an attitude, vis a vis liberals or radicals, much like that seen in the cowboys and Indians movies: where one good cowboy in a white hat could best or take out ten evil Indians barehanded before breakfast. Any conservative activist is sure that in a "sit down debate" setting, the liberals and their wishy washy liberal positions would be devastated.

What a conservative campaign loses complete sight of, is the fact that there is no desire on the part of the "other side" to establish the "truth" of some issue. The other side is interested in votes. A debate would only be considered if the odds were such that the results of the debate would be favorable to them. However, observe the following considerations, which may NOT be made by a conservative campaign.

Consider a debate between a conservative candidate for Congress and a liberal incumbent. First off, no incumbent congressman would consent to a debate in the first place, unless he felt horribly threatened by his reading of his polls. [We will disregard this for the sake of the argument here, however.] Let the debate take place in front of the county bar association with the media in full attendance: Subject: National Defense.

The most probable reaction on the part of the conservative's campaign, upon hearing that the congressman will in fact debate, is that the debate will allow the candidate to make a high score against the congressman. Accordingly, for about a week and a half before the debate, most resources of the campaign manager and candidate are focused on preparing for the debate. A campaign appearance is actually dropped the night before the debate so that the candidate can do his final homework. For one more time, he is going to pour through copies of *Human Events*, *U.S. News & World Report*, some articles clipped out of the *Wall Street Journal*, and one or two *Reader's Digest* articles, which have been assembled to "get some facts and numbers."

The debate format is such that each candidate gets 15 minutes to make a prepared statement of his position. Five minutes are allowed to make a rebuttal, and then there will be questions asked of each man by a committee set up by the association for the debate.

The conservative candidate, Jones, starts the debate by reading the first paragraph of a Wall Street Journal full page advertisement from September 8, 1977, called "The cult of Vulnerability Endangers the United States," reprinted from the September 10 issue of TV Guide. It starts out: "There is a cult of vulnerability in our country today, a never-never land of political thought that is as dangerous as it is naive. Its followers would have us reduce our military defenses to provide more money for unproductive giveaways, weaken our economy to pursue unattainable environmental goals, sap our political strength to further their muddled ideas of social progress . . ."

Jones continues on by citing various statistics on the relative positions of Russia's armed forces versus those of the United States. The numbers become a litany of armed might on the one side versus a decline in the position of the other. In every case the army, tanks, surface combat ships, attack submarines, tactical aircraft, ICBM's, strategic missile submarines, and bombers of the United States had declined in the face of ever faster rising numbers from the Russians.

Jones finishes his prepared portion by showing how the congressman has consistently voted with the liberals in the Congress to gut the defense budget and pare back what forces the U.S. had. Jones cites a couple of bills that the congressman has voted on to "prove" where the man stands on the "issue" of national defense.

Then, the congressman takes his turn. He does not dispute the figures or the voting record at all. He starts by saying that his "well intentioned" challenger had listened too closely to General Curtis LeMay back in '68 when LeMay was ready to incinerate the Vietnamese. Jones' presentation would have made LeMay feel very good, according to the Congressman. Furthermore, the lists of numbers of armies and tanks sounds like something the Conservative Caucus was always wailing about. Of course, the congressman would say, it was possible the challenger really believed "all that stuff." Also, the congressman felt sorry for the challenger who had obviously "bought in" to what the conservative direct mail kings were pumping out in order to get contributions from the gullible. He wondered, did Jones send in his contribution? (There would be laughter from the audience, and Jones face would get redfaced.)

When Jones gets his turn to rebut what the congressman had said, he accuses the congressman of avoiding the "issue," of making light of a deadly serious threat to the nation, etc. When the congressman takes his turn to rebut, he says the real "issue" is that there are too many Dr. Strangeloves in the country trying to scare people. He then asks why Jones does not address himself to the fact that there are 1,500 pounds of explosives in the U.S. arsenal for every man, woman and child on the planet. That, the U.S. could wipe out every town and village in Russia with over 5,000 in population. The congressman finishes by rhetorically asking whether the American people should allow a small bunch of Pentagon hardliners to be allowed to threaten mankind with more Hiroshima-type pyres; whether the threat of genocide is not a greater problem than the direct mail profits of the Conservative Caucus.

When the debate is over, one or two attorneys sympathetic to Jones' side go up to him, pat him on the shoulder, and say, "nice try, but you had a tough opponent. All things considered, you held your own."

In the context of the campaign in the district, the account of the debate in the next day's newspaper is not better for conservative Jones. The head line read, 'Congressman Smith Calls for Pentagon Efficiency." The article finishes up with the congressman's observation that last week his conservative challenger had been calling for the budget to be balanced, now the challenger wants to add $25 billion to the budget for defense.

Jones had gone into the debate with a notebook brimming over with articles, facts and figures. He had been prepared to talk about the Russians cheating on the SALT treaties. He had been prepared to debate the utility of the B-1 bomber versus the ancient B-52's. He had been prepared to talk about many, many more things than ever came up. He felt that in preparation, anyway, that he had won the debate. What Jones did not know was that the congressman had smooth position papers and statements his staff (from the Democratic Congressional Campaign Committee) on more than twice the facts and figures than Jones would have even thought of.

Challenger Jones had no conception of the juggernaut of

money, manpower, and depth of materials his own week and a half collection of conservative articles were up against. Had Jones accidentally been able to "get to" the congressman on a certain particular, such as the need for B-1 bombers, the congressman with his materials could have beaten Jones on Jones' own ground and premises of cost, efficiency, and devastation power on a "dollar for dollar" basis.

So, what is the net result, or bottom line, for such an exercise? Clearly, the debate took up much precious time from Jones' campaign. Clearly, in this hypothetical instance, Jones obtained precious newspaper space for his opponent, the congressman! An incumbent is "news" because they hold the position. A challenger has yet to prove anything at all.

A campaign MUST evaluate potential exposure versus the cost to get that exposure. In the terms of this example, how many lawyers at the debate could conceivably have been convinced to vote for Jones (compared to the way they would have voted anyway). Then, if only some tens of numbers of votes were possible to change (assuming Jones were to score a knock out, as highly unlikely as that would likely be) from the debate, what is the possible exposure from the media covering the debate? If the local paper is inclined toward the liberal congressman, its options are to: 1. not cover the debate, especially if Jones were an orator likely to best the congressman, 2. Include a sentence or so, "Congressman Smith debated his opponent at the county bar, yesterday," or, "Congressman Smith smiles at Jones assertions," or, "Bar Association has congressional race debate." 3. Give the debate a write up of 2 column inches, unlikely to be seen by the general readership of the newspaper in the opinion section (with one-twentieth the readership of the funny section). So, the bottom line from Jones' perspective is that he spent a week and a half preparing for a debate that took him away from contacting people who could vote for him. This was in order to *hope* that he might get some exposure from the local newspaper (because 10 more votes from lawyers don't add up to what the winning number of votes must be).

SI.

Or, even more starkly, if Jones did nothing more with his time than join the postcard volunteers writing postcards to the addresses on the precinct lists, in just over a week, he could have addressed nearly a 1,000 postcards, asking for a vote.

The point is obviously not that conservatives cannot win or that truth and commonsense cannot win. Nothing is further from the truth.

The conservative Jones (representing sincere candidates) in the example above would probably have been agreeable to a whole series of Lincoln-Douglas type of debates. He would have thought that this is the essence of democracy. Yet, even after such a series of debates, how many voters would have in fact been contacted? The people who stayed home watching "All in the Family" reruns, or new episodes of "ER," would still decide the election's winner.

The business of campaigning is strictly to find the number of votes necessary to win. The business of campaigning is not to try to best someone in a debate, whether the debate is before a group, in the newspapers, or in brochures.

Real Issues

A district inventory will have identified most interest areas in the district. It is from these interest areas that the issues for the campaign will come from. A candidate and a campaign will only seek to identify what local issue, or two, gets the attention of the voters. First, issues, which the candidate discovers from his/her meetings seeking influential support, are carried over into other meetings. Second, those issues, which are identified as of interest on the part of local voters, will be used in brochures.

Several "real life" examples, here, can illustrate the *real* use of issues. Consider how the professionals use "issues" compared to "idealistic" challengers. Television station KPIX in San Francisco carried a series of programs in 1976, called "Meet the Candidates," which aired a five-minute film of each congressional candidate in the surrounding congressional districts. The films were done on the "turf" of the candidate. All the candidates had to do was to prepare their material for the five-minute film.

On the evening of August 29, 1976, the viewers saw three incumbent Democrat congressmen give their five-minute talks, along with their three Republican challengers. The three incumbents were extremely liberal. They were Phillip Burton of San Francisco, George Miller of Martinez, and Fortney Stark of Oakland. They were the professionals.

The first congressman came onto the camera, talking to the reporter. His mood was calm and relaxed. The image, which came over ever so strongly, was warm, friendly, and avuncular. This image was starkly contrasted with what followed, that of his Republican challenger. The viewer's first impression of this person was of seeing an angry man in the Republican. It was not a *friendly* person who came on and started accusing the friendly congressman, who had just been seen, of various evil acts, deleterious to the country. Speaking fast, looking grim, and sounding strident were the challenger's accomplishments. On a person to person basis, a viewer would probably wonder, "how could a nice friendly looking man, like *we just saw*, possibly do all those things that the unfriendly, rigid looking and angry man was accusing him of . . ."

The next congressman came on camera. This one talked of what help he would try to continue to be to the district. He did not do particularly well in his own right. He was only a one-term congressman at that point. He did not do well until his challenger came onto the camera for the next five minutes. This challenger, also, came on strong by way of accusing the Congressman of doing destructive things to the country. However, this challenger was not as strident in appearance as the first one. The problem, nevertheless, was that this time the challenger was trying to go into great depth about things like inflation, eco-freaks, and morality (in less than five minutes). Not only that, but he used some "fifty cent" words in his 'airing," which few listeners

SL.

probably understood. Then, he finished up his time by touching upon the religious needs of the country. Just from the tenor of the presentation, many viewers could have felt uncomfortable in watching such a performance.

The last segment of the program put the third congressman's challenger on camera first. What viewers saw, was an ordinary looking "Joe" come onto the screen wearing sunglasses in the bright sun, from the time of day when the footage had been taken. After some serious sounding comments about the Vietnam War, (which had been over for more than a year), the challenger picked up his four year old son. He then went on to talk about how bad the future of the country would be . . . unless people like him were sent to Washington, right away. The more the challenger talked, the more unfocused he became (still holding the four-year old), and by the end of the commentary, the challenger broke down and had to wipe tears from his eyes as he choked up from contemplating what the world was coming to.

The congressman of the district was next. Refreshingly relaxed, in major contrast to the grim performance of the challenger, the congressman smiled warmly into the camera. He too had children in his scenes. After a few passing comments about the kids, the congressman started telling how much he had helped the district. He had gotten funds to help widen an interstate highway through the middle of the district. He told how many social security checks he and his staff had traced for the poor pensioners who had finally come to him for help. He recounted what he could do for families, when military transfers were about to cause a problem. In short, the image presented was that of a man who was in control and who was really concerned about the people in his district.

Parenthetically here, in each case above, the Republican Party was supporting the challengers with only token help. It was token help designed to keep the men from complaining too loudly about not getting any help from the party. The congressional seats involved in the Bay Area were considered to be "safe" Democrat seats.

It may be said in defense of the challengers that they were not experienced in the use of television, and that they could not be expected to do well. However, it must be remembered that these men were challenging the incumbents on political ground. It could be said, "If you choose to challenge someone on their ground, you should know the weapons likely to be used." Yet, inexperience aside, it was readily apparent that the object in the minds of the challengers was to hit the incumbents with "issues." Whereas, it was also readily apparent that the congressmen were there to ask the voters to vote for them—and they did so by appearing to be a "good" guy.

Many sincere candidates would scoff at the idea of being so transparent as trying "to smile" one's way to Washington or the state capital, or even to the school board. However, armchair ideologues never consider that the candidate must be liked by the people to get their vote. A political candidate does not need a stable full if "issues" to get votes.

In fact, a very successful politician in California became one of the few women to be elected to statewide constitutional office, as Secretary of State. March Fong used only one "issue" to make herself known to the people statewide, period! She had been a state Assemblywoman from the 15th Assembly District in the suburban East Bay. (For statewide recognition, she might as well have had a district next to Oregon/Nevada in Northern California.) Yet, with only one issue, she led the Democrat ticket in the whole state, the year when Jerry Brown was elected governor in 1974, succeeding Ronald Reagan. March Fong campaigned by letting the state know that she was the author of statewide legislation outlawing "pay" public toilets. She had "helped the little people out there." And, the voters bought it.

History has long ago forgotten an obscure mayoral election in Rapid City, South Dakota, on April 8, 1969. However, aspiring candidates for almost any office throughout the U.S. might do well to remember that race. Challenger Jack Allmon beat the incumbent mayor, Henry J. Baker, that day. As the *Rapid City*

Journal said on the front page, the next day, Allmon had "won a surprising first-round victory."

Of course, predictably, the reporter from the *Journal* article reported that Allmon's campaign had "centered on the issues that people were talking about," and that those issues had to do with "some concern over the state of affairs at city hall." However, observers of elections know that such statements are always the case. Fortunately, the reporter did report what was actually behind the victory. Challenger Allmon had pointed out the obvious. The roads in town had potholes in them, he said. When elected, he promised, *he* would get the things filled in.

During the race, Allmon had made an "issue" of potholes in the roads. The mayor countered by saying that under his administration, the city had spent more money than ever on new and better roads for the city. Yet, what the mayor and his administration never caught onto, was what every person who drove into Rapid City from the nearby Interstate highway knew. They had to pass through the city's busiest intersection, which slowed all transiting cars, because of a gaping pothole, square in the middle of the intersection. It was in fact very vexatious and hazardous to drive through that particular pothole. Allmon merely let the people knew that he would fix the darn thing. And, the mayor chose to deny its existence, as an "issue."

Issues should be considered to be subjects that get the attention and interest of the voters, or that of influential people whose support is being courted. Ask former Congressman Charles Wiggons of the California 39th District. Elected in 1966, Representative Wiggons received his biggest and most spontaneous flood of mail from his constituents in the early 1970's. The flood of mail was not on the "issues" of the day as seen in the newspapers on the editorial pages. The people who wrote were irate, because they believed that environmentalists were about to close the sand dunes in a desert area used by recreational vehicles. The people were moved to action because the "dune-buggy issue" hit them "where they were coming from."

On another front, some years ago, Congress had enacted legislation forcing auto manufacturers to put in a "seat-belt interconnect," such that a buzzer in new cars would not go off until the seat belts were buckled. Some of the heaviest mail ever sent to Congress, over an extended period of time, had to do with the profound unpopularity of that "interconnect." The law soon got "revised."

To the degree that a political candidate can find and identify with something that is readily perceivable as a nearby (and readily understandable) "wrong" or "need," then that candidate might have an "issue." This assumes that there is a believable solution, which could be brought about.

In the context of the type of campaign discussed here, a candidate must have at least two types of issues to work with. One type can be used for the "public" side of a campaign, potholes in roads, for example. The second type of issue is for another part of the campaign.

Issues for Influential People

The second type of issue is the kind used for an approach to influential people. As covered in the chapter on organizing, lunches or other types of meetings were to be solicited in order to meet and talk with influential people in the district. Information gleaned from such meetings could be used to further the process with others.

A district inventory will provide a candidate with ample understanding of the area, so that intelligent questions can be used to stimulate "Mr. Influential" to talk. Mr. Influential will most likely be interested in talking about his interests, which he believes coincide with those of his company. If he were a vice-president of a paperboard company, for example, he would probably be interested in talking about the prospects for the company. He would become community spirited in the context of talking about the beneficial impact of the company's payroll on the local area, etc.

This type of information can be put into a political context by the candidate in understanding the sphere of the company's influence. Other contacts and conversations by the candidate later, when discussing the area's economics, will be substantially more credible for having had first hand contact with information, such as Mr. Influential gave (without referencing Mr. Influential by name, obviously). Credibility is the key word. The goal of the meetings with influential people in the district is to get their support. That process is a cumulative one, as the meetings continue over time. The trade-off, however, is that a candidate must appear to be legitimately interested in the district, its people, and particularly (for support purposes), its businesses. [A politician who monopolizes a conversation by showing, among other things, his erudition in knowing how many billions of dollars were squandered by the Federal Department of Housing and Urban Development, is not anywhere near the "wave length" needed to relate to ANY district's people.]

The following ideas present some legitimately good questions to consider asking any Mr. Influential. Or, perhaps, while not asked as a direct question, nevertheless, they are good points of departure.

These are some of the questions, which the Fantus Company used in its reports for businesses. A president of the company at the time, Maurice Fulton, gave a talk to the Ninth Annual Statewide Legislative Tax Forum of the California Chamber of Commerce on March 18, 1975. The Fantus Company had an international reputation as a business location consulting firm (actually, *re*location firm). Mr. Fulton talked about business climate and the elements that make up such a climate. One category of the company's analysis was called, "state taxes, programs, and laws affecting business." Under this category, the company asks the following questions:

"How heavy are the taxes in a state?"

"How stiff are the unemployment compensation and worker's compensation laws?

"How committed is a state to big government and to big government services?

"How large a public assistance load has the state undertaken?

"Are unemployment compensation laws and worker's compensation laws administered with an eye toward economy?

"How extensive is the governmental structure of the state?"

A candidate or campaign does not need to do any research of its own into answering such questions. A candidate need only know such questions to ask in order to find out what real, honest-to-goodness issues are in the area—from the people who are in a position to know by virtue of being on the "front lines."

The above questions, regarding business climate under a regulatory umbrella are examples which, with the right emphasis and "spin," can be used by candidates anywhere from congress to candidates for the local school board. "Relevancy" is the keyword.

A campaign, which comes to realize that the meat and substance of "issues" is what really counts to the people of the district and in the district, will take a major step forward in its quest for finding and getting the support of influential people. The poignancy of what is "real" in issues can be seen in the following letter from Robert C. Benson Jr., director, Portsmouth Economic Commission, New Hampshire. Mr. Benson wrote to the *Wall Street Journal* after the *Journal* had stirred up a hornet's nest of controversy by comparing the economically progressive policies of New Hampshire with the statist regression in Massachusetts.

"Your editorial on New Hampshire (Jan. 4) is instructive if only because it poses a question that Massachusetts has consistently refused to address. The state has, to its misfortune, chosen to provide services instead of jobs. This choice causes taxes to skyrocket, resulting in an economy drained of strength. There is little statewide growth of significance foreseeable—the best hope is a holding action."

"In all this, there is cruel irony. As the state sought to meet public needs by expanding government services, it ultimately deprived the public of its greatest need: an economy capable of growth and the opportunity for a healthy job rate. Had the state chosen economic development—jobs—as its priority, the need for so many social programs—and the taxes to finance them— would never have reached present levels. Those who work have little need for Massachusetts' social service programs."[54]

A political candidate in Massachusetts at that time, who understood the proper use of issues, potentially should have had influential supporters standing in line to help! By pressing the right nerve, a political campaign can find out the relevant information it needs for issues in gaining influential support. This can be done at the same time as the support is given and votes accumulated. The campaign only needs to ask the right questions. If the query is sincere, information will pour forth by the people who are forced to deal with large headaches by having to have direct contact with government—at all levels.

Consider the problem of industrial development of land. While most areas will not be as bad as the San Francisco Bay Area, nevertheless, the potential for seeing good examples of what makes for good issues, is readily available. Again, "issues" in this context are for the courting of influential people, not necessarily for publishing in mass brochures.

There are eight major permit-granting agencies which have responsibilities, i.e. jurisdictions, legal authority, criteria for decision making, processing times and steps in reviewing business permits. These agencies are the Bay Area Air Pollution Control District, Bay Conservation and Development Commission, California Coastal Commission, Department of Fish and Game, Regional Water Quality Board, State Lands Commission, State Water Resources Control Board, and the U.S. Army Corps of Engineers. Also included are the California Environmental Quality Act and the National Environmental Policy Act which deal with environmental impact reports.[55] Any business involved with any of these agencies will, almost by default, get involved with the others. Further, without a central clearinghouse for permitting, the possibilities of getting into very frustrating situations are immense. Hence, there is obvious transformation of an action (or non-action as the case may be) into an issue.

Each state and political subdivision has its own problems and governmental hierarchies, fiefdoms, and spheres of influence. The listing of these layers of government in a district inventory by the campaign, as each is discovered, will lead to other groups of potentially influenced people (through their contact with the agencies) and other real issues.

It is by this process of discovering government and business interaction where-by candidates at all levels can seek out the "natural" interests in their political subdivisions. Then, the natural "issues" to those interests can be discovered. For example, a prominent attorney in a race for a seat on a hospital board in 1978 had been solicited by two board members to make the race for an open seat on the board. The attorney never thought to sit down with the incumbents to find out what the "interest pressure points" (issues) of the race might have been. Ambulance company executives in the area were not talked with—to discover what their concerns were. Neither were administrators of other hospitals in the area contacted. Consequently, the candidate had no knowledge of substance to offer influential people in the area as to why they should support him.

It is in the light of understanding what *real* issues are, that the emptiness of much tub-thumping of standard conservative issues can be understood. Too many conservatives love to trot out the absurdities of $342,000 granted by the federal government for Michigan State University researchers to ask college students where, when, and with whom they had had premarital sex.[58] Or, the study for $100,000 for mailing sex information and condom stamps in unmarked envelopes to lists of teenage boys considered sexually active, with the price per package of prophylactics totaling nearly $400.00.[57] Or, the Consumer Product Safety Commission, which spent $142,000 on a study which determined that most injuries occurring in bathtubs and showers were the result of "slips and falls."[58] In the sense of stimulating the interest of a person/voter in a candidate or the campaign, the foregoing are not "issues" at all.

Issues from the Ancients

A parenthetical note on the problem of understanding the substance of issues is in order here. This is to show that the misunderstandings about what issues really are, are long standing, to say the least.

The orator Synesius gave a renowned oration to the feeble Roman emperor Arcadius in 398 A.D.[59] In the oration, Synesius touched upon the issues of his day. He lamented the declining morality of the people, the declining defenses of the empire in the face of the Barbarians, and the need to arouse an interest in the people to defend their laws and property. However, in the language of Gibbon, Synesius "had not condescended to form a practicable scheme" to right the ailments of the society which were so readily perceivable.

The degeneracy of the Romans had been progressive. Military legions, which once had made most of the ancient world tremble, were emasculated by giving up the weapons and armaments, which had made them nearly invincible.[60] Not too many years before the fall of Rome, the Imperial government was bestowing honors on the soon-to-be conquerors of Rome: Alaric, who ultimately sacked the city of Rome, was named as a master-general of the Roman armies. From the vantage point of being part of the defenses of the empire, Alaric had the defense industries of the time "provide his troops with an extraordinary supply of shields, helmets, swords, and spears; the unhappy provincials were compelled to forge the instruments of their own destruction."[61]

One final comparison from the decaying times of the Romans to current times is instructive from the point of view of understanding the ubiquity of "issues."

"The freedman of Onegesius exposed, in true and lively colours, the vices of a declining empire of which he had so long been the victim; the cruel absurdity of the Roman princes, unable to protect their subjects against the public enemy, unwilling to trust them with arms for their own defense; the intolerable weight of taxes, rendered still more oppressive by the intricate or arbitrary modes of collection; the obscurity of numerous and contradictory laws; the tedious and expensive forms of judicial proceedings; the partial administration of justice; and the universal corruption . . ."[62]

Being Right

From the standpoint of a political candidate engaged in a political contest, the above comments on decay and degeneracy are equally apropos of current times. However, just as the comments did not help when they were made, so too, the same comments now are of no political help. A political campaign wins no points for making accurate comments or commentary on the current state of affairs. Being "right" on the issues and losing the election is the same thing as an automobile driver demanding his "right" to drive through a green light when a Sherman tank is running the opposite red light. Or, as Jim Murray asked in an article in the *Los Angeles Times* some years ago, while your constitutional right may be to walk through Central Park in New York City at midnight, do you really want to exercise that right? A person needs to be able to collect his "rights," or they are worthless. A campaign must collect votes, or all of its efforts at being "right" on issues are meaningless.

Cassandra was right in warning of the dangers of the Trojan Horse. However, she gained nothing for having been "right." In fact, instead of being celebrated for having been right, her name is only a synonym for warning in vain of evil—with a sense of noxiousness combined. She happened to be "shrill."

Closer to our own times, during the 1920's, Sir George Paish was a famous financial advisor in Great Britain. In March of 1929, he was quoted in several publications, including the *American Literary Digest*, regarding the bad state of affairs of the world economy.

Paish said, "We are threatened with the greatest financial disaster the world has ever known." He was right, but all that his efforts gained him at the time was the opprobrium of the *Wall Street Journal* and the *Washington Post*. Both papers disparaged his comments. They did so before the October crash and subsequent depression. Sir George was right, but so what?

A campaign, which spends much time or resources in researching issues of the day in order to make neat newsreleases (quite often for sending to hostile media people) will most likely reap the same rewards as the prophets mentioned above. Time is so short and resources so sparse, that a campaign needs to focus on vote gathering. Just because issues are almost universally misunderstood, there is no excuse for a campaign, which wants to win, to get caught up in "issues."

Media Issues

A campaign will be using a limited number of issues for the public side of the campaign, and then, only when necessary (something needs to be put into the campaign brochure). Also, a campaign will be using issues of substance in its search for the support of influential people.

When a perception of success greets a campaign, a closer scrutiny of the campaign will take place at which point one or two issues may be required for the media.

In the pursuit of its goals, a campaign, which is doing a good job of contacting people and asking for votes, will become widely perceived as being an active campaign. It will gain stature. As the potential of winning becomes greater, the media will take an interest in the campaign. The state of affairs will become apparent to the media that the campaign is moving forward and doing something different. The media will also become quite curious as to what is going on, because there will have been substantially less contact from such a winning campaign than from other campaigns. (Losers have traditionally tried to curry favor with the media in the mistaken idea that publicity can be gained from "media courting.") The media is going to try to find out more about the campaign, and in this process the campaign will come under demands for stands on the "issues."

At this point, a candidate's contact with influential people in the district can be translated into one or two overriding themes. Certainly, any issue, which was identified through the meetings with influential people and which has come up several times, would be a local issue.

Before spotlighting the issue by way of newsreleases, the campaign would certainly check with the influential people who had pointed out the issue. Many times a local businessman who was the focus of unfair governmental action would welcome publicity, but other times it would be entirely inappropriate.

A fast way to create interest in a local issue is to create a "trend." A newsrelease would begin: "If current trends continue, the 9th Congressional district will lose 1000 jobs in the _____ industry because of _____ regulations, Walter Jones, Republican candidate for Congress, stated today. Citing figures from the industry, Jones noted that the industry had lost 500 jobs over the past two years . . ."

This is real news and something only the most biased news outlet would disregard. The media can follow up on the candidate's allegation, if it wants to. Furthermore, since the information came from the industry itself, the credibility of the candidate is greatly enhanced. Such releases must avoid appearances of being from *that* industry's "own" candidate, however. The thrust of the release is the candidate's concern for the well being of the people in the district.

Candidates for contests for school boards, hospital boards, etc., should be able to identify some issue in the district which can be "trended out" (extrapolating current trends would lead to X or Y results). Most people are surprised to see the changes in personnel numbers, payroll size, or number of people involved in practically any business over a ten-year period. Any person can find the figures on one of these points from ten years ago, get comparable figures for the present, and then make a projection. Of course, any candidate, before doing such a release, would necessarily check with a knowledgeable person (an "influential person") in that business BEFORE going public with such projections. This is why such "issues" must come from repeated contact with the people who know about the area of being focused on. Such issues cannot be grabbed from out of thin air by a paper candidate or campaign.

This approach to the use of issues for newsreleases is natural. The hard work of seeking out influential help and fund raising will pay dividends in issues. The knowledge and concern of the candidate for the district will be communicated to the people who are watching. Generating newsreleases is not a primary function of a campaign, however.

Spheres of Influence

Most conservatively inclined political activists get a liberal "fix" on a legislator and proceed from that point in doing battle with her or him. "He (she) is a liberal, therefore . . ." What most such "fixing" fails to understand is that the sphere of contact of a legislator is very wide, indeed. A legislator who votes for increased welfare funding, increased personal taxes, and other liberal programs has not, ipso facto, lost the elements of support out of the community, which may be thought to be conservative, particularly on the business side.

Many conservative activists fail to understand the "reality" of a situation in which a business finds itself. Any business, which is impacted by policies of the political subdivision in question (in the district), is going to be sensitive to what happens within that subdivision. In many communities a "prominent" Republican can often be found to be supporting Democrats. For instance, in one county a quite prominent Republican would not help any state legislative candidates. Statewide candidates and national office seekers got quite visible support, but it did not trickle down. The reason was that the man was a CPA with a substantial amount of business coming to his firm from the county administration, tied closely to the Democrat local establishment. The county administration could be tied closely with local state legislators. Obviously, all the "issues" which local Republicans would work up, would never budge this person.

The same thing is seen on the part of many businesses under, what conservatives would consider to be, "hostile" legislators. A business in such a situation is not interested in issues, except those that would perpetuate business and serve to keep it "hassled" as little as possible. If this means buying hundreds of dollars of tickets to the local union council fund-raising dinners, so be it. This is even if someone (a conservative candidate or supporter) were to point out that the funds would be put into political action accounts to further the power of liberal politicians. A typical answer to such an observation would be along the lines of, "you've got to get along."

That such a situation has been widespread is seen in contribution figures from businesses to incumbent Democrats. This has been even when the Democrats were substantially more liberal and supposedly antibusiness, as opposed to Republican challengers. Democrat incumbents received 46% of the campaign funds disbursed by business in 1976. This was taken as a sign that business played to incumbents. In the first 10 months of 1977, Democrat incumbents got 75% of contributions made.[63]

Obviously, something more than "issues" has been at stake. Either that, or the issues which are of importance to business are being taken care of. If such is the case, then business is probably using a narrow definition of its own interests. However, even in view of this, no "education" campaign by a candidate for political office is going to make a marked change. A conservative candidate wishing to score in such a situation must walk gingerly to find out what is *at* issue. In many cases, since the businesses have been making their accommodation with the political structure, they become oblivious to the chances of change by having no contact with the opponents of the power structure. Clearly, businesses are not idealistically courting liberal versus conservative votes "on the issues" and "exercising their best corporate citizenship."

The magnitude of such accommodation can be seen in the following example. In 1976, in a state legislative race in the 14th Assembly District in California, there was a doctrinaire conservative running against an equally doctrinaire liberal incumbent Democrat. The Democrat had demonstrated his political expertise by rising quite fast in the power structure of the state Assembly. To any interested observer, the stance of the incumbent on "the issues" was very clear. However, a sizable newspaper, the second largest daily in the district, endorsed the Republican challenger. The endorsement pointed out that the challenger was more in tune with the district than the incumbent.[64] The endorsement also pointed out the incumbent's many anti-business votes in the legislature.

Yet, consider the following list of business oriented groups, which contributed to the incumbent: Wine Institute Fund $250; California Optometric Political Action Group $200; Importers Political Action Committee $250; California Home Furnishings Council $200; Life Insurance Political Action Committee $250; Coalition of California Apparel Industries $250; Diversified Personnel Services $150; Peterson Tractor Co, $50; Machinery Credit Corporation $50; Manufactured Housing Institute $100; California Life Underwriters $300; California Grocer's Association $200; Cargo Pac $500; Kaiser Aluminum and Chemical $200; Warner Bros. Inc. $350; Motion Picture Association $300; Board of Realtors Political Action $200; California Automobile Dealers Association $500.[65] With only one exception, there was virtually no contact on the part of any of the listed business groups with the conservative challenger. The contributors were merely buying "access" to the incumbent.

In most cases, funds are sent out strictly because a person is an incumbent. It is readily apparent, therefore, that "issues" in the mind of most conservative activists play an extremely narrow part in the political decision making (calculus) of businesses or other groups, when their interests are involved.

Such accommodation is probably, or should become, an issue in and of itself. However, the same question pertains with this issue as with virtually any other issue. That question is, "how many votes will it get?" or, "how large a contribution will it get?" These are the acid tests for an "issue" in a campaign.

Such a calculated approach to issues will inevitably be criticized by the "uninitiated" as being cynical. Any idealistic conservative who falls into this trap and who doesn't subscribe to the preceding arguments should consider one last test for "issues." The people, who don't know as much as a campaign position paper outlines on an issue, probably don't care about the issue. Those who know more about the issue than is put forth in the brochure will not be swayed away from their established position by less information (what is in the brochure). Further, anyone interested, beyond the two approaches already covered here, has probably seen the arguments before, anyway. Therefore, what utility can there possibly be in pursuing an "issues" avenue? Utility in the context of a campaign is only measured in money and votes.

Polls

Polls have not been suggested for campaigns here for the obvious reason that the basic campaign outlined here does not depend on "issues." The district inventory and the search for influential support both supplant the need for polls. Also, the use of a local issue is more in tune with the interests of the voters than trying to divine the level of interest in a political matter.

The financial realities of polling are usually too great for a local campaign to even consider polling. However, a campaign should not feel guilty if the subject arises. Quite simply, the money for a decent professional poll could be better used in other ways in the campaign to ask for votes, not opinions.

Some congressional races and larger state legislative races may feel pressured into doing a poll to lend credibility to their races. If a PAC is interested in a race, but the lack of a poll is holding back financial support, do the poll! This is if the results of the new support (contribution) will offset the added costs of doing the poll, obviously. If the campaign has the services of a bright, energetic, college student with statistical abilities, who will do an amateur poll, okay. There is a methodology in the Hal Evry book. [30]

However, not even all professionals swear by polling. David Garth commented about other campaigns: "A lot of people pick their issues from polls." Not him. "If you think something—say, education—is a serious problem, then make it an issue."[66] Political strategist Kevin Phillips disparaged the polls taken by Pat Caddell for Jimmy Carter, saying that "everything depends on the way the question is phrased."[67] A basic campaign, as outlined here, is not traditional and based on "issues." It is designed to win.

Yet, some people will not accept the fact that "issues are not relevant." There will inevitably be pressure from some part of a campaign, which feels that a major opportunity is being lost by not pursuing "the issues of the day." Should this pressure mount to disruptive levels within a campaign, it would be best to let the pressure off by having some "letters to the editor" done by the people who are pressuring for the use of issues. Since there are usually several types of publications available in a district, which entertain such missives, let the people involved make their own campaign of such letters. These can cover transgressions of the incumbent or whatever the object of the "issue" might be. However, let the "pressurers" use their own time, not that of the campaign.

In summary, issues do not come into a campaign from the editorial pages of newspapers, magazines, or the good intentions of supporters. Issues must be considered in the light of the district and inventories made of the district, first. The handling of issues must be considered in the context of the available time and resources at the disposal of the campaign after the basic "ask for the vote" campaign has been implemented.

10

Media

A campaign will use media in a supportive or supplemental role to the basics of campaigning already outlined in this work. The foundation of the campaign will have been laid with the public and private methods of asking for votes and help. The media tools can then be used to reinforce what is already taking place in the course of campaigning.

The form and substance of the campaign should not be confused. The substance of the campaign is people. People asking people to vote for the candidate is the essence of the campaign. The more personal the manner in which the contact takes place (through friends, influential people, postcards, etc.), the more substantial the campaign is. As the campaign widens and needs to reinforce its communications with the public, media will be used.

Brochures

The most basic trapping of a political campaign is its brochure. The brochure in and of itself establishes the fact that there is a campaign taking place. A brochure is the business calling card of a campaign.

So long as the campaign remembers what it is doing, the brochure need only be very simple in communicating who the candidate is and what the campaign is about. Bearing in mind that the interests of the person who is looking at the brochure are of paramount importance, the brochure will try to convey its relevance to the district.

Pictures from around the district with people from the district are the best ways of establishing relevance. The district inventory will have identified the important areas in the district. The pictures in the brochure, therefore, of important areas in the district will communicate to the reader that the campaign is aware of what is important.

A standard six-paneled brochure made from printing both sides of 8–1/2 x 11 paper is the best because people are familiar with it. A truly large number of pictures can be put into such a brochure with room left over for some short comments on one or two important issues. One panel of the six can be used for the "who is John Jones" biographical part. People want to know who the candidate is, but beyond a certain degree, they lose interest in knowing every last thing the candidate has done. The key word is relevance.

With modern speed printing and offset machinery, a campaign does not need a tremendous amount of lead time or a professional photographer to produce a useful brochure. A person with some experience in shooting pictures (as long as the focus/scene of the photo fills the frame of the picture) can make good 35 mm photos and take them to a one hour developing establishment. One day with the candidate and photographer can produce enough pictures from around a district to put a brochure together, so long as it has been well planned. A couple of changes of clothes for the candidate for serious, relaxed, and sporty types of shots will break any monotony of the photos. Appointments with influential people who consent to being in the brochure can be planned and taken with a minimum of disruption for the principals involved.

The layout of the brochure can be done either by the campaign steering committee itself by arranging the pictures on a mock-up, or by having the help of the printer at the "quick-print" shop. Or, there are usually many free-lance graphics artists available who could do a good job (almost anyone in business will know of a graphic artist). An advertising agency is not necessary merely for laying out a brochure.

The brochure should be thought of as a living document, to where additional printings will almost certainly be done, especially if some highly influential people down the line would sign-on with the campaign and consent to being in the brochure. Having widely known individuals in the brochure as "endorsers" is just plain good politics. This is obviously done by changing panels in the brochure to accommodate new photos.

Consider having a picture of a prominent contractor and his wife standing in front of a half-finished house. The type to be set for the picture would merely say, "Jones believes the free market can provide housing needs. Mr. & Mrs. Brown agree." When Jones gives copies of these brochures to his contractor supporter, that supporter and his wife will certainly be interested in passing out the brochures and encouraging people to look through them. There will be a personal interest in passing out such brochures, which would far and away transcend the altruistic notion of passing out plain brochures "for good government." [It should go without saying that the decision to include a given supporter in the brochure is a kitchen cabinet decision.]

The same position in the brochure can then be filled in with a picture of a doctor supporter looking at the tongue of a cute little girl with the caption reading, "Jones believes doctors provide better medicine than government." The doctor and the family of the little girl will certainly be interested in passing out such brochures.

This device can be used with perhaps 25 very influential people throughout the district. So long as it does not appear that the pictures are obviously additions strictly to butter up such people, they can be effective. The basic brochure will be using many pictures of many people in order to get a "people-orientation" message across. The campaign might as well get as much mileage out of the pictures and the brochure as possible. A campaign, which had planned sufficiently far enough ahead, could have produced a considerable number of such brochures using a large number of the people who would later participate in the "one day finance committee" day. The flexibility of fast-printing techniques gives a campaign good latitude with proper planning.

It should not be misunderstood that the above device is to take the place of any other parts of the campaign. This is a supplement to the seeking out of support from influential people. It is a way of facilitating an influential person passing around that he/she is supporting the campaign.

A campaign with the financial resources, which has made the decision to have the candidate walk certain precincts in order to reinforce the post-card campaign, may have many printed up for passing out.

Graphics can become a bone of contention when making decisions on the campaign's basic brochure. Color, style of print, and "artsy" layout often incur haggling over what is best. Price should be the determining factor for brochure color and whether or not color photos will be used (most likely not, certainly not for the substituted photos in printing several brochures).

Senator Carl Curtis at the 1974 Conservative Political Action Confer-ence in Washington D.C. summed up his ideas of brochures by advising "lots of colors and pictures." The campaign will want to use the same color theme on the brochures, if color is used, as the color sniping signs used through out the district. The candidate will be well advised to choose two or three color combinations of warm colors and let the steering (kitchen cabinet) committee choose. Everyone has ideas as to what colors are best, but even the professionals will get into a box from time to time. A seasoned professional politician running for U.S. Senator in California in

1976 used an ugly yellow on light-green for his brochure. However, the only thing color can do for a candidate is to reinforce the feelings of the people toward him, one way or the other. With all the variables in election contests, anyone who thinks colors will rescue a losing race or lose a wining race is kidding themselves.

The style of print and the layout of the brochure should be focused on what is really important, election day. Instead of having the first full panel of the six in the brochure used up the standard, full face bust shot, with the trite, "coat over the shoulder, loosened tie" shot of the candidate, a smaller picture and three or four ballot-type-print logos approximating the ballot appearance of the name, would be better. The viewers of the campaign materials would be farther ahead from the campaign's point of view if they have seen the final day's printing of the ballot name several times. Not to dent the egos of graphics professionals, but the style of type will do nothing to gain votes for a campaign. The style can only lose a chance for positive reinforcement if it is too artsy/stylized or cluttered. Legibility and simplicity in type and format will serve the campaign best.

A Bad Example

An example of a bad campaign brochure can reinforce points made here. A man running for the Houston City Council in 1972 passed out a legal sized piece of paper with narrow margins, chock full of printing in all capitalized words. Within the narrow margins, he crammed in over 1,500 words on the one page. His picture and a very cluttered heading made it hard to decipher who he was, or what he was running for. It turned out it was for "district C." There was no schematic map indicating what district C was, or even a few words indicating what geographic section of the city it was. [While the Internet was not in vogue in 1972, a reader's reaction, then, to a page of all capitalized letters in words was the same as 1995: "netiquette" on the Internet says that all-"caps" is the equivalent of screaming.] Upon reading the copy, it turned out that the candidate in fact knew what he was talking about. The really unfortunate thing was that the clutter of so many words and the all-caps print stopped most people cold from even attempting to wade into the copy. [It would have taken little imagination to come up with photographs of some of the more egregious problems the candidate alluded to and to space out the copy—into a couple pages. Form and substance are equal from the point of view of making an impression.]

He hit on the problem of the duplication of various City of Houston and Harris County services. A photo of the duplicate tax offices, put next to each other, with simple copy about cutting out the duplication, would have been effective. The candidate also hit on the problem of pornographic smut being available to children on the city streets. A picture of a child (staged) about to put a coin into such a vending machine could have demonstrated the problem. It could have been captioned, "Your child? Get smut off the streets!"

The candidate also hit unsanitary conditions in many restaurants and the need for new health inspectors. This could have been attacked with a photo in the rear of some greasy spoon type of restaurant. It could have been captioned, "Have you ever looked BEHIND your favorite restaurant?" In short, in a six panel brochure with pictures (for not much more cost), the communication with the voters by way of the brochure would have been expanded markedly.

Almost needless to say, there was no mention of any supporters in this particularly bad example of campaign literature. Several names, if not pictures, should have been included. Otherwise, the candidate has not connected himself with people in the community.

Calling Cards

There is another type of literature, which can take the place of brochures from time to time. This is the standard sized business card, 2 x 3–1/2 inches. People are used to receiving a business card and many times will save it in a stack with other cards. They are not programmed to toss them away to the degree they are political brochures. A standard sized business card can have a one-inch square photo of the candidate, even 1–1/4 inches square, printed on it. This leaves enough room to print the name (similar to how it will appear on the ballot, the district, and one or two short phrases. The utility of such cards becomes apparent when meeting many people in a large gathering and having something to give to them to reinforce the meeting. Having a bunch of campaign brochures might be inappropriate or cumbersome. The cards are very inexpensive, comparatively, and many different people supporting the candidate can be given the cards at no great expense. These are called "people cards."

Direct Mail

Hal Evry, the top flight advertising professional, in his book, *The Selling of a Candidate*, says that direct mail is one of the two most effective means to impact the voter. Sniping signs are the other. The use of direct mail is a decision to be made based upon the financial resources of the campaign. With the basics of the campaign taken care of, direct mail may be considered. Since voters are already being asked to vote for the candidate personally by postcards, direct mail drops will be used to reinforce the credibility of the candidate by using endorsements of either a few well known backers or many people who are not public names, preferably, both.

A letter, which is signed by several influential people stating positive reasons why they are voting for the candidate, is one type of letter. The letter can be to the effect, "In my business, it's tough to make hard decisions. One decision I know that will be good for our district is to get John Jones into Congress . . ." The more the district is covered by the influence of the individuals signing the letter, the better.

There is a second type of letter to send, a "we support Jones because . . ." form. Included with the letter would be a page of signers. The page of co-signers would be broken down by town, city, area, and other divisions of the district. Five to ten names minimum from each subdivision would be sufficient for each person receiving the letter to want to look through the names in search of ones they would know. Fifty names minimum should be considered for this type of letter. Again, the whole idea behind this approach is to amplify the "people support" of the campaign.

Direct mail is effective in hitting issues also, but the issues should be those discussed in the section here on issues. A particularly effective picture can be included, for instance of potholes in roads, should that be an issue. It is just as important to include many names, which agree with the point of view of the letter. This heightens the credibility of the issue.

The drafting of the letters and the points of view conveyed should be decided by the kitchen cabinet because it will be a cabinet-wide job to get the endorsing names for the letters. The actual physical production of the letters, the addressing, stuffing, and stamping, can be handled by the postcard group of volunteers from the same mailing lists of precincts. The chances of a hand-addressed piece of mail being opened and read are much greater than a labeled envelope. So long as time is available, the money saved, by the campaign doing the mailing versus a professional house doing the mailing, will get that many more pieces out.

Signs

The use of sniper signs and lawn signs has already been discussed in the basic campaign plan presented here. This is a footnote on typestyle. The idea of the signs, is to impact the voter for election day. The signs need to be kept simple—with simple type style and simple message: the fewer words on the sign the better. The last name and the office sought are the only prominent words necessary. A substantially smaller first name is best. Avoid slogans on the signs.

Remembering the goal of the signs will help to avoid getting too much copy on the sign face. The sole purpose of the signs is to make the campaign publicly visible. It is the number of lawn signs that are significant, not the message. It is the ubiquity of the sniper signs, which make them significant.

Billboards

Unless billboards are obtainable in significant placements, it would be best to avoid worrying about them. The lead-time necessary to contract for a billboard showing, and the money necessary to guarantee placement, are often too early in the campaign to be realistic for planning purposes in view of funds. If the candidate, or some influential person, can obtain from the billboard company, through personal friendship, prominent billboard placements, for example, those facing major highway arterial exits, then a billboard campaign might be worthwhile (assuming the funds are available). But without significant reasons for using billboards, they should be avoided.

Campaign Letterhead Stationery

While most major statewide campaigns do it, too few local campaigns do it. This is the listing of influential supporter's names on the left side margin of the campaign stationery; the more areas and the more names, the better. Many campaigns feel that listing "worker bee" workers in the campaign from different areas of the district is good for the campaign. It may be. However, there is usually little to be gained from the point of view of recognition of names by using nice, but not well known, people.

Also, the production of too much campaign letterhead stationery is to be avoided. Follow-up notes sent to influential people after candidate meetings can be done on smaller paper than office sized stationery. Actual campaign literature will be printed up especially for the occasion. Therefore, campaign communications on its letterhead will often be limited in number.

Campaign-Media Relations

As in so many other areas of campaigning, the relations of a campaign with the newspaper, radio, and television professionals in the district are rife with misunderstandings. The creation of a campaign does not automatically create interest in it. In looking at a campaign, media professionals will consider the same things as political party professionals. The media is not swayed by a sincere sounding candidate, or an enthusiastic "press secretary." The media will often ask a candidate how much he or she thinks they will spend in the race for the seat. The media will also ask who in the district is supporting the candidacy. Idealistic comments about the "plans" of the campaign really have no particular meaning or ability to get the attention of the media pro's.

Many campaigns feel that courting the press and electronic media will somehow get more attention than otherwise. Certainly, good human relations are a must, but that only makes for a level playing ground in relations. It does not make the relations. What is misunderstood by many campaigns is that the credibility of the media is involved when it covers a campaign.

Consider the following actual endorsement from a well-known daily newspaper for a likely loser in a state assembly race. In an editorial, "Our Assembly Endorsements," the newspaper acknowledged: "Political reality—the most visible sign of which is the lopsided Democratic registration in each of the three districts—tells us that the incumbents will win reelection handily." However, nevertheless, once stating that it was aware of the situation, it recommended a Republican opponent of an incumbent by stating that it felt the Republican was closer in tune with the district.

It finished the endorsement by saying: "a generous vote for [Jones] will tell [Smith] to move away from the liberal fringe of the Assembly. We think such a message to him is long over-due."[68]

The community in which media is situated is its ever present audience. Which- ever the media, print or radio or TV it is a part of the community. The executives of the media are often part of the community and have interchange with people in the community. They cannot afford to go overboard, or even appear to go overboard, for a campaign and end up looking foolish for it. A medium, which starts to lose credibility, will start to lose advertisers.

The message for a campaign is that once it has started to make an impression on the community in which it is working, then, it can start to expect some attention from the media. The better the prospects for the campaign, the more interested the media will become. The more money a campaign has, the more interest the media will have. It will sense that it may get some of that money in advertising revenue.

As in anything else, it takes accomplishments to garner attention. Merely being a campaign or a candidate is not sufficiently distinguishing for attention beyond basic acknowledgments.

On a positive note, the by-word in dealing with the media should be professionalism. The business of the media is knowledge: knowing what is going on in its territory. If a campaign keeps the media posted as to the progress of the campaign in the light of "for your information" news-releases, the media should respond equally professionally to the campaign. Once a campaign becomes "real" by virtue of a rising interest level from the district and other manifestations, then a campaign should expect to be treated professionally in return.

There is a school of thought among many campaign professionals, which advocates sending newsreleases to the media as often as possible. This has prompted some foolish campaign efforts. One such was a West Coast congressional candidate who had his staff send out one news-release per day to the surrounding media. To this day, the campaign manager of that campaign is proud of the fact that his team did such a good job. Observers of the same race often wondered what the campaign was up to, because there was hardly any notice in the newspapers regarding the campaign. Quite simply, the candidate and campaign were not credible to the media. All the avalanche of news-releases accomplished was to line some waste paper baskets. The efforts put into the news-releases included some quite high-powered Republican National Committee help, also. In this case, the releases were professional, but because the campaign was not considered to be a winner, the releases were disregarded. Just plain common sense says that a campaign must be perceived to have substance in some aspect, before it can command attention.

Voter Impact

It has been reiterated several times that media may be used by a campaign as a supplemental feature to the campaign basics outlined here. The reason for this can be seen when considering the efficiency of the media in impacting the potential voters of a district. The "impact area," readership in the case of newspapers and viewership in the case of TV, etc., of each medium will likely be either substantially larger than the campaign's district, or substantially narrower in interest scope than the campaign's potential voter.

Even the district of a congressional race is often smaller than the scope of some of the media, which are in it. In such a case, the campaign would be paying to impact people who are not even in the district. In other cases where the medium is wholly within the district, the interests impacted by the medium have got to be considered. In a primary race, where the conservative is a Republican, it could be questioned how effective advertising on the local country and western radio station would be. Some estimates would have to be made as to the registration of the likely listeners, their ages, and their propensity to vote in a primary election. Most radio stations have a close idea as to their demographics. Ask them.

A general idea of the demo-graphics of the district and the impact of the medium should be not too hard to "hand massage" into some rough idea of the size of the bang for the buck expended. That is, the likely number of voters impacted. The obvious points for such an approximation are to be considered along with another point, an interest and attention paradigm. The ideal voter, for a campaign to attempt to impact, is the voter who is about to vote and who is asking him/herself or acquaintances, who to vote for. The time is right, the attention is there, and the interest of the moment is on the election race. The constant repetition and reinforcement which the campaign has tried to accomplish throughout the campaign outlined here, is designed to break into the interest and attention span of the voter. The use of media advertising is a very blunt method when considering the odds of catching the voter in a receptive mood. Hence, the constant and expensive repetition of media advertising.

When a campaign steps into media advertising, it is competing with the professionals promoting commercial goods. Newspaper ads for the campaign will compete for the attention of the reader against "cents-off" coupons, sales, and other advertising. Radio or TV commercials will compete with the announcers selling cars, or furniture, or TV's. Certainly, a campaign can hire its own advertising professionals. However, a low budget campaign will get low budget professionals. Slick ad agencies will have their best people on the best commercial accounts. Also, many top agencies will not deal with a campaign, which is not apparently likely to win for fear of damaging the ad agency's reputation.

Advertising Agencies

There are several considerations to make when a campaign decides to hire advertising professionals. In the rush of the typical campaign, the sales arguments of smaller public relations firms selling their advertising skills are often persuasive. Their basic point is that the campaign does not have the expertise or resources to make newspaper ad layouts, do the desktop publishing, and make the insertion-purchases in the papers, or other media, smoothly. Likewise, the lack of campaign expertise is even more pronounced when contemplating radio or TV commercials. It is also said that the rates charged by the media will be the same to the campaign, whether the campaign does its own work or not. That is, the agency gets a commission when making a placement, which the campaign will not get.

In so far as billings for space in a print medium or time on electronic, it is usually correct that there is no additional cost for placement (the 15% commission comes out of the cost). However, this begs the question of the fees charged by the ad agency for its creative work.

It is in the areas of political knowledge and creative efforts that the campaign and the ad agency will come most often to grief with each other. The agency feels its knowledge of dispensing ideas is greater than a "recently put together" group of people assembled and now called a campaign. After all, with its expertise in impact, the ad agency can get "the" magic talisman over to the voters, which will swing the election "once they know." It is at this point that the whole problem of "issues" will rear its predictably ugly head.

The creative efforts of an ad agency are its stock in trade. Should a campaign not like the approach, offered by the agency to put across an idea, the agency could very likely feel like it was kicked in the ego.

These two problems, combined with the possible incursion of the agency into the affairs of the campaign, tend to lessen the desirability of using an ad agency for smaller campaigns. The suggestions, which follow on media advertising, can be realized without the use of an ad agency, for the most part. This is not to condemn ad agencies or indicate that there is no room for them in a campaign, which obviously not true. Yet, the trade off of fees paid for help than can often be done by the campaign is a major decision in view of the efficient use of each dollar for voter impact. Just as the whole field of media use is predicated upon the basic campaign having been already implemented, so then too, once the dollars are available, the thought of streamlining certain efforts with the use of an agency can be entertained.

Advertising

There are two basics or fundamental factors which advertising efforts must deal with. The first is that the advertising must be people oriented. This means the advertising should feature people supporting the candidate. The people will be both influential people and some "just people."

The second fundamental for advertising is the necessity for getting attention for the ad or commercial. The terms for getting attention in a newspaper ad, which is competing with the soap coupons, are to use extremely wide borders of white space. An extreme application would be to use a three quarter page newspaper advertisement which had one sentence in the middle of the page: "John Jones is my choice for Congress because he is best for the people of Stanleyvill, Smithville, and Lakeside. Joe Smith, owner and president, Smith Truck Lines." In terms of using radio, attention is gotten by the use of several different voices saying the same thing, or even using children's voices. Stopped action on TV will draw attention.

It will be noticed that issues are not used in the above. The "people idea" in the campaign's advertising is the same as in its public and private voter contact campaigns. Advertising need not pander by using words such as "everyone" in order to create the bandwagon effect. The idea is always to pound in and reinforce the number of people who are talking about voting for Jones.

Technique

Just as a district inventory was made to find the important areas in a district, and a vote inventory was made to find where the votes must come from, so too, a media inventory must be made. This is nowhere as time consuming and involved as the other inventories. It also provides a reason for the campaign to have contact with the different media.

Quite simply, the media inventory will identify what the media are in the district . The daily newspapers, the weekly newspapers, and even legal newspapers in the area should be identified. Getting their circulation base and ad rates are important, as is getting their deadlines and contact persons. The same information is necessary from radio stations and TV stations. The commercial rate schedules of the radio and TV stations will be most interesting from the point of view of the drop off of in rates from prime time to non-prime time. This can often be exploited by the campaign.

A campaign, which wishes to place a newspaper advertisement, need only know the above information and then ask an advertising representative of the newspaper how to get the ad in the newspaper. As long as the campaign knows exactly what it wants to say, the fact that the campaign does not have an ad agency to make the placement will not stop the advertising salesperson from the newspaper from getting the ad into the paper and getting the revenue for the paper (and the commission). The representative will tell the campaign that the ad department can block out the ad with a week's notice, (or something similar). A campaign can rest assured that the newspaper will tell the campaign how best to get an ad into the paper. Just ask.

The best types of advertisements for newspapers are the one sentence type mentioned above using a very influential name. They get considerable attention because people are drawn to the one sentence in the middle of all the white space. The next best people-type of ad is the space full of names, often from one particular interest group, showing the support from that group. Of course, getting the names is a project in itself, but the dividends are paid off by virtue of an extremely high degree of credibility. This can only come from a long list of names backing the campaign.

Radio commercials can be approached in the same manner, as above, in so far as generating the spot is concerned. The station may not have a department, which would produce a commercial within the budget of the campaign, but the station can suggest people in the area who could help. However, there is one nice thing about radio commercials, which a campaign can take advantage of. It has been suggested here that people-type (people intensive) commercials are the best. With this approach, a campaign need not pay for "talent." A reasonably savvy person, who has a pleasing voice and who can project with it, can be a lead voice in a series of 30 second spots of a series of voices all saying, "John Jones has my vote for Congress." A good cassette tape recorder and some practice in putting the voices on the tape can produce some thoroughly acceptable commercials. Radio stations, up to the 50,000 watt size, have their own reporters using cassette tape recorders.

Again, an advertising representative of the radio station will be more than pleased to advise a campaign as to the requirements necessary to get spots onto the air. The only final qualification that must be made with "do it yourself" radio commercials is that the campaign let the effort rest for a day, and then listen to it critically before moving forward with its use. The enthusiasm of the production could color a poor performance. If it sounds good the "next day," go for it!

Television must be approached more gingerly. The visual demands of viewers need to be met professionally. The equipment necessary for TV spots precludes must amateur attempts. However, the spread of community cable TV stations has opened channels for "do it yourself" TV ads. For extremely reasonable rates, a cable TV studio and equipment can often be used to produce tapes, which can be used by commercial TV Again, a campaign should work closely with an advertising representative from the station for professional tips and mechanics. Of course, the radio spot "idea" of waiting for a second day to critically judge a spot holds, also.

Again, people are the important element in a commercial. Getting several people who can say, "John Jones is my choice for Congress," convincingly, is good. Getting a couple of influential people to appear in the spots is very good. People like to be wanted. If "Mr./Ms Influential" is willing, get them into a TV spot. It's not too much of a stretch to guess that he/she will let all their friends know to "watch Channel 7 this evening."

A suggestion for the spots is to simply have a group of people, close together, come into view, backs of heads to the camera. Then, one after the other turns around to say, "John Jones is my choice for Congress." The message over and over is that people are going to vote for Jones. The simplicity of the message goes far toward its gaining acceptance.

If Jones got into the commercials and condemned government waste, or the inflationary votes of his opposition, he is just one more politician throwing mud at another

The basic point to remember about media advertising for low budget campaigns, is that the effort is not to bring about a vote change for the candidate because of the advertising message. The point is get "presence" and to impress the district that the campaign is active. It is only another prong in a series of reinforcements of the campaign's activities.

Internal Advertising

There is another area which campaigns can use quite effectively. This is "internal advertising." In most cases the rate schedules of radio and TV stations have drastic reductions for non-prime time advertising spots. Time slots sometime during the 9:30 to 11:00 PM time frame are often available quite inexpensively. A program can be put on at this time to "use" the medium in order to get credit for being on TV. Many times people will take appearances on TV to be a substantiating element in the progress of a campaign. This type of program can be used by way of referencing in the postcard campaign, or a direct mail piece with a footnote: "Be sure to see Jones and friends on Channel 5, Oct. 6 at 10:30 PM." A fifteen-minute "program" can be done rather effectively with a *seasoned* interviewer (M.C.), who leads the candidate and several sup-porters in a discussion of the campaign, the candidate, and the district. Lots of names and place names should be used in order to put the candidate into the thick of the district.

A word of warning is in order, however, for this type of "program" piece. The program must be thoroughly planned out and it should have several backups for time fillers. Knowing that there is sufficient material to fill the time is a "must," if the program is to be done live. If local cable TV studios can be used to produce a good quality tape, then it would be best to take the pressure off of the participants by doing the program on tape ahead of time. People are all "experts" on what a good TV program is, but put them into one, and they will freeze, have their mouths go dry, or they will fidget. [It is not so far out to have a package of sour-tart candy for everyone to bit into, just before the red light on the camera goes on.] The absolutely unavoidable pre-requisite for such a program is an *experienced* interviewer [M.C.], who is experienced and comfortable in front of the cameras.

Just as an influential person, who appears in a TV commercial will make sure people are watching, so too can a campaign add to the size of the audience by having lots of people in such a special program. The extra people can be prominent business people, local candidates for lesser offices [than the one of the sponsoring candidate], or even a children's group to sing "You are my Sunshine" to the candidate. Each participant will generate viewers. Again, a word of caution. The group MUST be warmed up before going onto the program, even in the cable TV studio for taping.

They absolutely must be as comfortable as circumstances will permit, or they will come over extremely stiff to the viewing audience. Arrival at the studio a minimum thirty minutes ahead of time (with the doors barred for late arrivals) is a must. Then, having someone tell corny jokes to warm up the group really needs to be done. One grim person can sink the whole effort.

The beauty of such "people intensive" programming, at off-hours time, is that even if the most egregious mistakes are made, the size of the viewing audience will not be sufficiently important as to swing the election. The mileage for the campaign comes from having been on TV and letting people know about it. This is another "reinforcement" for a campaign's "people" thrust.

Non-prime time on radio will many times vary with the radio station. Some stations maintain that they have practically no "off hours." Prime time for radios is drive time in the morning and evening. However, stations claiming "no non-prime" are trying to indicate that their programming is so balanced that they get the housewives in the morning and the teen-agers in the afternoon with the senior citizens listening in during the evening. Fortunately, there are usually several radio stations in any given market. Some stations will have inexpensive time available for "internal" campaign advertising.

An overriding factor should be noted, here. That is, in media saturated metropolitan areas, it may not be realistic to use much newspaper or electronic media because of the tremendous over-reach into other districts.

This problem is often self limiting, however, through two devices. First, radio and TV may limit commercials, which effectively blocks out such advertising. Second, the prices can be high enough to make alternative types of advertising more cost effective.

News Conferences

A campaign should really not consider using such a device for getting out the word on something of importance to the campaign.

Forget news conferences, unless the campaign has something extraordinary to say, which is in fact a real scoop for the media. Media picks and chooses whether or not to attend a news conference—of incumbents, let alone challengers. It is best for challengers to avoid even attempting what could be construed as an ego trip, such as calling the media to come to the campaign for something newsworthy. It will save credibility for the campaign.

If a conference is in fact called, the campaign needs to be ready to parry the question on the telephone, "What's the conference about?" Answering that question will lead to the next question, "What's the candidate going to say." If that question is answered, the campaign will have scooped itself—and that media outlet will have no reason to show up. A news-conference where no media, or just one outlet, shows up, becomes negative news—no one was interested enough to come out, which shows how unimportant the candidate is. A campaign does not need this type of event.

11

Fundraising

Money provides the motive power for any campaign. As a necessary ingredient, even with ample manpower and time, money enters into most decisions of substance, which a campaign will make. Yet, finding, soliciting and obtaining funds for a campaign are probably the most painful chores contemplated by a campaign. This need not be the case. First, consider the traditional hang-ups held by ordinary campaigns. Then, consider what can be done.

Traditional Approaches

Most campaigns, from the size of a congressional race or smaller, start out poorly financed. Yet, many of the so-called experts on campaigning, belabor the obvious. Consider what the literature offers up: "Therefore, the ideal budget should begin with a large proportion of the funds raised in advance of much formal campaigning, yet make allowance for money raised later."[69] Equally as enlightening is the following: "One final word about money: get it early, get as much as you can . . ."[70] Or, even Hal Evry, in his peppery way, had a minichapter in his book, *The Selling of a Candidate*, which was titled, "In politics: It's no go without dough."

For most campaigns, naming a fundraising chairman is the beginning of the pain, not the beginning of the end of the pain. With fundraising usually only getting a slice of the "time pie," it is easy to push the unpleasant job of asking people for contributions to a back burner. Once a campaign comes to the realization that the fundraising chairman in and of him(her)self will not be able to work miracles, the campaign often retreats into setting up fundraising dinners, wine-tastings, and other social get-togethers.

The result of wasting much planning time and effort (which translates as "selling tickets to people") in setting up dinners, BBQ's, etc., is frustration. This comes from the expenditure of so much effort to receive so little in tangible results.

A typical fundraising mistake is to confuse an event designed to raise money with an event designed to get/ show popular support. A typical campaign planning session for fund-raising event will inevitably turn up a person with the bright idea of having a hotdog feed "for a thousand people." The bright idea is for the campaign to make a profit of $2.00 on each hot dog dinner sold, which would translate into a campaign event profit of $2,000.00. It's not until someone forcefully points out the degree of difficulty of getting a thousand people to come to an event, until reality comes to the campaign for that type of idea. [Two seriously interested influential persons could contribute $1,000.00 each to reach the same goal—and the effort to contact or find them would be seriously less than the efforts at trying to round up 1,000 people to buy tickets for a hot dog feed.]

However, typical planning for a "fundraising event" by a typical steering committee centers on the "right" ticket price for an event. One person wants a particular "social set" of the district to be the target to attend the event, another person wants the event not to "exclude" some good campaign workers, who cannot afford a high price for tickets. Such debate misses the mark. The goal of fundraising is money, not "thanks," strokes or bodies in attendance.

What complicates the problem further, is when an event is made into a publicly announced affair. An event which is to raise funds and which needs to come up with a large number of bodies, has doubled the target goal. Once a campaign gets itself into this box, it stacks the odds against itself. This is because it will be judged by observers of the event on both counts. If a campaign were to announce a massive fundraising picnic looking for 500 people, the event would be a dismal failure if only 100 people showed up. This would be the case even if those people contributed $100 apiece.

The extent of the problem of deciding ticket prices for events can be seen in the contortions in a West Coast congressional campaign in 1976. Secretary of the Treasury Simon (at that time) was to make an appearance for the candidate. The campaign committee tried to decide what to charge at the event. In a session of 17 people for the committee meeting, the discussion covered prices ranging from $25 per ticket to $100. It was decided to ask the Secretary's staff. The staff suggested $75. The issue was settled by the candidate, who stood up ceremoniously and announced that the price would in fact be $75. Furthermore, he said, he didn't want anyone who could not afford $75 at the function. Then, the campaign tried to let the tickets "sell themselves," believing that having a name personality would "sell" the tickets. The campaign "announced" that such an important person was going to make an appearance for the candidate. The campaign did not do any "armtwisting" of influential people to buy tickets.

The results of the lack of planning were disastrous for the candidate. It soon became common knowledge that tickets were being passed out in order to "get some people" there. This alienated the people who had laid out $75 in the first place. It also alienated the campaign committee, which had heard the imperious decision of the candidate. It further looked bad when the newspapers reported a total of 50 people in attendance for the U.S. Secretary of the Treasury, in from Washington D.C.

SL

The Secretary, who had just come from an overwhelmingly successful dinner in Cleveland, was mortified that so few people attended.

The whole problem could have been avoided, and a major success made of the event, if the campaign had had the goal of raising funds in the forefront from the beginning and proceeded on that basis. Had the event been private, and had the campaign billed it as an opportunity to meet with the Secretary of the Treasury in a private setting, then the tickets could have been $500.00 per person. The campaign would have been happy and the Secretary and his staff would have been happy.

This is not to say that campaigns cannot have fundraising dinners, picnics, or BBQ's in order to get lots of people to attend. However, the goal of the event must be clearly in the forefront and the main thrust of the event must be the overriding focus. Like everything else, which the campaign does, a calculation must be made as to how to get the biggest result for the effort involved.

A traditional method of approaching fundraising by a campaign is the establishment of a fundraising committee under the direction of a chairman. The idea is that the committee will have each of its members raise his/her share of the target amount. This is the "all-ya-gotta-do" school of fundraising. If the goal for the committee is $50,000.00, and there are 15 people on the committee, "all" they have to do is raise $3,400.00 each. "All" that takes is for each person on the committee to find ten people who will each give $340 or some combination thereof. Often in the enthusiasm of the moment, a member of the committee will write out a check for $500 to start the ball rolling. Invariably, most of the other members will have "forgotten" their checkbooks. One or two other checks may dribble in.

Along the way, one of the members will confess that he/she had in fact made a couple of calls to some friends to seek out the $340. However, he will say, the people always had good excuses for not being able to make the contribution "at this time." And "after all, you can't force people to give money."

The problem with such an approach to fundraising is the same as with any other endeavor without guidance. After the initial try, most of the committee gives up and thinks up excuses of their own as to why they can't get the contributions (and this is on the part of the 50% of the committee which comes to further meetings). Fundraising must be considered to be part of the total campaign and it must be approached on a personal basis. Fundraising should be pursued as efficiently as possible. This means going after contributions with as few encumbrances on the efforts expended for the contribution as possible, such as giving dinners, or what ever. However, guidance and organization are the bywords of successful fundraising. Parceling out the responsibility for fundraising to several people only divides the problems for follow-up. Or, conversely, giving the total responsibility to one person and then leaving it with that person is just as bad.

Snow White

One of the top professionals in politics in the '70's, Paul Newman (no relation to the actor), often recommended the use of the "Snow White and the Seven Dwarfs" approach to fund-raising. The approach is neat and simple. When done right, large amounts can be raised.

Snow White is the finance committee chair. Each of the seven dwarfs, committeemembers, becomes a focal point for fundraising after they have contributed an initiation fee. In many cases each dwarf hosts a breakfast, where the dwarf has invited the potential contributors, letting them know that the hosted breakfast is going to discuss raising funds for the campaign. For a congressional race, the "ante" for each contributor is on the order of $100 to $500 per person. Obviously, each breakfast is put together such that the financial capability of the individuals is similar.

The organization of the breakfasts is along similar lines with the committee sitting down together and planning the procedure, which each dwarf will use. In this way, each person is thinking of their own function, yet there is the camaraderie of doing the planning together. There is also a friendly competition, which will develop, as the time for the breakfasts draws closer.

A different approach with the same method is to have each of the committee members host a reception type of get-together for the contributors at a prominent home in the area. Again, each potential contributor is told that funds are to be the topic of discussion. When Paul Newman has discussed the approach for the reception type of function, he has stressed that the invitation for each contributor indicates "cocktails and black tie." The psychology of the very prominent home and the near formal dress lend themselves to the giving of funds.

The positive aspects of such methods for fundraising are that the goal is singular, i.e., the raising of funds, and the means are singular, contracting those who can make sizable contributions. In this manner, other factors do not obscure the very necessary search for funds.

In keeping with the central theme of this work on campaigning, which is multiple self-reinforcement of people-contact, there is another method of fund-raising. This type of fundraising will flow nicely from the work that the campaign has already done, elsewhere. The work on the district inventory and the ongoing search for contact with persons of influence can be used as a form of preparation for fundraising. The contact of influential people fulfills the preparatory work, so often needed in sales, before the sale can be made. In this case, the sale is the giving of contributions.

From the district inventory the areas in which to search for people of influence were discovered. Furthermore, when contact was made with the individuals in order to have a lunch together, or whatever, it was stated that funds would not be solicited at that meeting. Through the course of the lunch or conversation, the candidate solicited the knowledge and views of the person of influence. Also, there was the campaign follow up after the meeting. With that amount of contact, translating it into a donation should not be hard at all, so long as the approach is well done.

The Budget

Equally important, along with "approach" to fundraising, is the necessity of having a goal regarding the amount of funds to be raised. The kitchen cabinet needs to rough out an idea of the amount of funds it will take to implement the public and private parts of the campaign in order to get the necessary votes to win. Results of the vote survey of the district and the realization of the amount of work it will take to make all the necessary contacts will have matured in the thinking of the kitchen cabinet. Therefore, one or two reviews of the total campaign plan should crystallize a necessary figure for winning purposes. This is the goal. Add ten percent, arbitrarily, and that figure becomes the goal for fundraising efforts.

Community Chest Approach

It is a comforting realization: understanding that the campaign has already made contact with a large percentage of the potential donors to the campaign. This is because in many instances the people who have been large contributors in the past to other campaigns are the people who have an interest in the area, politically. However, depending on the approach, these people will often "buy their way out" with a $50.00 "buy-off," when being solicited for a contribution.

The same person, approached properly, will likely make a contribution at a substantial level, because they will feel as if they are contributing more than money to the campaign. In the author's experience, the following approach has yielded the most funds for the efforts involved.

Terry Weldon, a top professional in the Republican ranks (some years ago), refined the following approach from the old community chest fund-raising methods. Many people, on what will be the finance committee, have already seen such a funds campaign work. This familiarity helps also, and may add a refinement, locally, to the plan as presented here. It is presented here, briefly, in outline form. The goal for the plan, is $25,000 with the number of people involved for the duration of time indicated. Generally, the plan, as shown here, is about half of what a congressional race could do if properly implemented. The numbers can be changed in any way to suit the size of the campaign and other variables.

The outline:
1. The one day finance committee
—25 people take 1/2 day off from work
—Goal of $1,000 per person for the effort
—Make list of 400 names (prospects) for 16 contacts per person
—25 x $1000 = $25,000
2. Campaign committee functions
—Mail out advisory letter, "We will be calling."
—Phone call to set up appointment
—Plan and plot out map route for each person on target day
—Have packet of campaign materials for each person
3. Flow of events
—Night before target day, group meeting for briefing
—Target day:
      —Beginning lunch appointment
      —Appointments length by size of possible donation
—Phone contact: each committeeperson calls in each hour to give progress report and to find out how others are doing.
—Reception (evening of target day)
—invite committeepeople for cocktails
—invite contributors for the same
4. Advantages
—One day only—not dragged out
—avoids "painful" telephone calls and follow up on promises
—Wide participation, group participation, band-wagon effect

Commentary on the program:

Each committeeperson who will be making the rounds on the target day will supply his/her prospects to the campaign so that letters of contact may be sent out. Contact by the campaign will be made to verify the appointment, and the planning of the route that will be taken.

The hardest work to be done entails the work by the finance chairman recruiting the 25 committeepeople. Yet, in most cases the candidate will have already spoken with these people in the search for influential support or spoken to a close personal friend. Knowing that this program will be used by the campaign facilitates the planning, also, by both the candidate and the finance chair.

Finesse in the drafting of the letter to be sent out is necessary. If the finance chair is not in the kitchen cabinet, he/she should attend the meeting when the letter is drawn up because it will be a letter over his/her signature.

A major undertaking by the campaign in time and manpower will entail the matching up of the appointments of each potential donor in order and by route for the committeeperson who will make the rounds. Again, proper planning is necessary.

The advantages of this type of approach to fundraising should be apparent. Everything is planned ahead. Everything is a group endeavor, with the positive reinforcements that come out of group efforts. The group morale in watching the unfolding of such a project will add to the enthusiasm of each working member, heightening the results. Finally, the entire project is dollar oriented. All efforts are centered on the efficient acquisition of funds.

Initial Campaign Funds

The approach outlined above for fundraising, is obviously for a campaign, which has matured in its travel toward election day. A problem which all campaigns have is how to get seed money to set up shop. There are two methods, among many, which could be considered. First, a campaign can rely upon the "big splash" method of targeting a couple of individuals who are close to the campaign and then impressing those individuals with the sincerity of the initial efforts of the campaign as to enthusiasm, hard work, etc. A request for a realistic donation "to help us get started" can be made.

Another method of getting a significant amount of money in order to implement some of the initial goals of the campaign would be to seek loans from a few individuals. There would be an understanding that the loans would be repaid out of the results of the "one day finance committee" operation outlined above. The signing of a note by the candidate would probably be necessary. This is also a way to enlist a couple of committeepeople for the "one day finance committee" in order to work on their loan repayment. This, however, need not be broached until the creation of the committee. Seeking much more than ten per cent of the goals of the "one day committee" in loans, however, could be hazardous and possibly counterproductive.

Special Interest Money

There are many fine organizations around the country which contribute to campaigns, which are aligned with the goals of the particular organization. These are political action committees (PACs) set up by many businesses and wealthy individuals through out the country. However, the guiding fact of life regarding getting contributions from PACs is that success breeds success. In other words, money begets money.

It is totally unrealistic for a candidate or campaign to make any sort of overture for getting actual funds from PACs, until the campaign has shown some meaningful action. "Meaningful action" in most cases means money in the campaign treasury, unless the candidate happens to be very prominent in the area.

Mere philosophical alignment of a candidate with the philosophy of a particular PAC is not particularly meaningful until actions of substance can be shown and demonstrated to have taken place.

A virtual campaign in its own right will often be necessary in order to make a realistic approach to PACs for funds. These would need to take place in three areas. First, the campaign must make its presence known to the PAC. This must be followed up with a campaign of courting the decision-maker of the PAC with attention. Second, the courting will need to take the form of sending copies of newsreleases and other publicly generated materials. The PAC will need to see positive results that the campaign is making public headway. Third, the PAC will need to see that the campaign is helping itself by raising significant amounts of funds. PACs help those who help themselves.

Only after the three steps from above have been attempted and successfully carried through will it make any difference to show a PAC the "plans" for the campaign. It is often amusing for campaign professionals to see the importance which amateurs place on having a written campaign plan which shows what the campaign is "going to do." Most campaigns, which try the "campaign plan" approach to success in money raising, fail to realize that there are hundreds of other campaigns "out there" with grandiose plans for what the campaign could do with vast amounts of money.

Steady contact showing steady success will be the best indication of the "reality" of a campaign in the eyes of a PAC. A real campaign, which is actually moving forward in its efforts, can be effective in raising funds from PACs by the above methods with one added ingredient. This is to keep PAC "prospects" abreast of planning for the one-day finance committee program (or other fundraising progress). A campaign can keep the PAC abreast of the progress with a "footnote for communication" with the PAC along the lines of, "once we have raised the $25,000 from our program, would you contribute $xyz? If the courting of a PAC has been realistic, some sort of commitment could be touched on, based on a successful one-day finance committee event.

In short, the route to successful fundraising is the same route as the rest of the campaign. Keeping in touch with the reality of the people, the district, and the campaign is the best guideline. Campaigns do not assume a stature any larger than the people and successful efforts in them. Homework, planning, and organization need to become apparent to observers. Success breeds success.

12

Information

Even as candidates pursue the type of campaign outlined in this work, nevertheless, they will find that they must be informed about the "issues of the day." This is because it is expected of political candidates. In seeking influential support, volunteers, and votes, candidates still have to demonstrate that they are aware of, and have a position on, many "issues."

The problem for a candidate and campaign is one of time and money. A campaign simply cannot follow "all" the issues. While a district inventory will give solid guidelines as to the most relevant areas for campaigning locally, a general overview/ knowledge of current affairs is still necessary.

Suggestions

The following are suggestions for campaigns and candidates with a conservative "view." Issue awareness and taking positions for a candidate usually take two forms. One form is knowledge of what is going on. The other becomes a position statement. The second is a more formal outline of a position with cogent arguments and a delineation of points.

[A strong attempt has been made in this work, in the chapter on issues, to dissuade a campaign from getting into the time and resource waste of formulating position papers. This sort of activity is best indulged in by statewide campaigns and/or well-financed campaigns. However, if a campaign insists on doing position papers, the sources recommended in this chapter can make for cogency and efficiency in formulation.]

[Another aside, regarding sources of information is in order. Since there is no single definition of the word "conservative," many who call themselves such will take a different tack on a given subject/issue. The working definition used in this work is that a conservative is one who subscribes to the classical liberal positions espoused by the founding fathers of the U.S.A.: limited government and free enterprise. These are the basic foundations on which a conservative rests.]

The unfortunate internecine warfare that goes on between conservatives is usually on the battleground of government interference in social matters. Some conservatives see a greater role for government than others do, in regulating social behavior.

With this in mind, no claim for consistency between the various sources listed here is being made. However, each source can be valuable in its own context. Even such homogenized intellectual hash as offered up in *Time* magazine can be used from time to time.

Periodicals

For a general grounding in current events and issues of the day, *U.S. News & World Report* and the unabashedly conservative, *Human Events,* are quite sufficient. While *U.S. News & World Report* can be in the liberal camp on some issues, nevertheless, its format and style leads its articles to be very "usable." This is in the sense that its articles purport to give both the current state of an issue and also backgrounding. Further, the magazine tracks issues coherently and individually "packaged" in two and three page articles. Therefore, for the uses recommended elsewhere in this work, especially for giving speeches, *U.S. News & World*

Report's headlines are without peer. Quoting *U.S. News & World Report* to an audience is allowable as an "unbiased" source, even begrudgingly from liberals. What is particularly good is that articles usually have facts, figures, and statistics, which are considered authoritative.

For example, consider the headline for an article in the 9–25–95 issue of *U.S. News*. The headline is self explanatory: "Does Bilingual Teaching Work? In practice, a good idea often gone wrong." A candidate wishing to discuss bilingual education can use this sort of headline quite easily to start a discussion. The important thing is that the authoritative headline takes away the need to *establish* the truth of what the headline says. If someone wants to argue with the "truth" of the headline, cited above, let them argue with the magazine. This leaves the candidate free to move on to what he/she would do about the problem and how to benefit the citizens in the district.

However, quoting a headline from *Human Events* would be immediately impugned and attacked as ideologically "biased" by a liberal opponent. *Human Events* makes the following statement about itself: "In reporting the news, *Human Events* is objective; it aims for accurate presentation of the facts. But, it is not impartial. It looks at events through the eyes that are biased in favor of limited constitutional government, local self government, private enterprise and individual freedom." The newspaper follows Congress closely and carries tallies of roll call votes in the House and Senate on important legislation. It is a "must" for conservatives to stay informed.

Business Publications

For candidates whose campaigns are working on a district inventory and also working on the "influential people" identified in it, the daily *Wall Street Journal* is excellent for keeping up with current affairs. Also, for fine "business, issue by issue" coverage on a weekly basis, *Business Week* is a must. Especially so, are the special reports which *Business Week* does regularly. Reviewing past issues in a local library for any special reports, which have been done on industries, which may be in the local district, could be highly productive.

A note in passing may be worthwhile. For campaigns using an "influential person" approach for electioneering, business information from any source can be considered to be for "intellectual gambits." As the dictionary defines gambit as "a remark designed to open a conversation," a candidate (who won't have time anyway) need not try to memorize every article in any publication. Merely being able to ask, "Did you see the article in yesterday's *Wall Street Journal* about falling interest rates," is quite sufficient. Again (as shown elsewhere in this work), the headlines from these publications will be the most useful parts of the publications for a campaign.

However, as good as the *Wall Street Journal* is, and it's probably the best, a busy candidate will usually not be able to keep up with a daily perusal of the *Journal*. For business discussion purposes, *Business Week* fills the bill just nicely. With a weekly magazine, a candidate can keep up quite well with what the mainstream media is discussing as to what the most current business "issues" are.

With a modest "stable" of only three weekly publications, a candidate and a campaign should be able to stay fully abreast of "what is going on."

Newsletters

While there are many good political newsletters available, demands on time are just too great for a candidate to try to assemble and assimilate too much information. This is another reason for the strong emphasis on an "ask for the vote" type of campaign, as opposed to an "issues focused" campaign.

When dealing with newsletters, and the favorite monthly subject of the writer/author, a candidate/campaign needs to ask the tough question, "what bottom line, practical, good" will come out of this information source for the campaign?

Surprisingly enough, the *Rush Limbaugh Letter* just might qualify as a useable source of information for a campaign. This would be in two areas. The first is in the sense of giving well researched information on selected "issues" each month. The problem is that with only a couple of highlighted themes, a campaign would need many back issues to cover the same number of issues which would be touched upon in a two month collection (9 weeks)of *U.S. News.*

However, it is in the second area that the Limbaugh letter is just great. Every month Limbaugh has two full pages of "Stupid Quotes." The quotes are fully referenced as to the person and the media in which they were reported. The lines are not only good for reading as entertainment, but they are good for spicing up speeches.

Opposition Research

In the area of opposition research, for partisan races, the political parties at the relevant levels can provide materials. For nonpartisan races, the results of the "district inventory" discussed in *Campaigning* will be appreciated as a basic foundation.

In partisan races, the relevant party legislative caucus will be the place to start for opposition research on incumbent opponents, or those who have previously held elective office. In other words, for a congressional race, the party caucus in Washington D.C. will be a source of the most cogent information on incumbent legislators. For a state legislative seat, the party caucus for the particular house will have the information. For example, for a person running against a sitting Democrat assemblyman in California, the Republican Caucus in the Assembly in the state capital, Sacramento, would be expected to have the most up to date information on the voting record, etc., of the incumbent.

One of the reasons for the approach to campaigning suggested in this work is that it avoids the seductive idea of finding "chinks in the armor" of the opposition.

In *Human Events' booklet, The Conservative Action Guide,* each U.S. representative is rated according to the rankings of conservative and liberal interest group organizations. The five organizations are the American Conservative Union (ACU), the American Security Council (ASC), the Americans for Democratic Action (ADA) and the Congress on Political Education (COPE). In looking at the ratings of a knee-jerk liberal such as Democrat Ron Dellums in the California 9th District, the ratings are predictable. Dellums' ratings from the March 10, 1995, issue of *Human Events* (the ratings which are used in the Action Guide) were: 5% out of a possible 100% by the ACU with a cumulative career voting rating of 6% out of 100%. His rating by the ASC showed 0 out of a possible 100%. On the other hand, his rating by the ADA was 100 out of 100 with a lifetime rating of 100. His COPE rating was 93%.

The same sort of rankings can usually be found at the state level for state legislators. Rankings will usually be done by the state chamber of commerce regarding levels of support for business backed legislation. Then, there will be environmental and other groups, which give their interest group ratings, also.

The problem with "report card" types of information is that the "other side" can usually counter with an opposition organization's rankings. Often, such organizations have been specifically formed to blunt the ratings of a given interest group.

A liberal politician may practically never support what would be considered to be a "law enforcement" position as represented, for example, by a "State County Sheriffs Association." Hence, that politician could get a low rating for "law enforcement support." However, it is possible that something like a "State Sheriffs Research Organization" could be set up by a liberal faction to give a high "law enforcement" rating to liberal politicians.

In nonpartisan races, information from the district inventory will lead a candidate to "interested" people who would know "where the opposition is coming from." Probably the easiest and quickest way to "get a fix" on the opposition is the old tried and true method of "birds of a feather flock together." The key element is to find the knowledgeable and authoritative people who can identify the "birds."

Quite often, the county headquarters of the political parties will have files on incumbents and potential candidates who have held other elective offices.

Focus

It is of the utmost importance to keep a focus on what information is sought out and the reasons for getting information on the opposition. Opposition research is time intensive and often time wasting.

Searching out scandalous material is an extremely hazardous proposition and most likely to be counter productive. Furthermore, digging up dirt on the personal life of a politician is waste of time. "Hit piece" campaigns are outside the scope of this work, especially since the public is getting increasingly tired of political mud and negative assaults. Stooping to the lowest common denominator of mud slinging usually involves high cost, slick, direct mail and high-risk campaigns. This is all in direct conflict with the tenets of the approach in *Campaigning*.

If a campaign is put together around a district inventory and "influential person" approach, then getting positive support from the interested people of a district should take care of itself.

The Internet and the World Wide Web

The development of the World Wide Web ("Web") as an information source is historically unprecedented for its utility in enabling campaigns and politicians to get their message out. The "Web" (not to be confused with the existence of the Internet) did not exist for the 1992 campaigns and it was not a factor in 1994, because it was brand new. This had all changed by 1996.

Nielsen did its first survey of the Internet in 1995, concluding that 24 million Americans and Canadians, aged 16 and above, used the Internet over a 3-month period. Other surveys indicated that one third of the U.S. population owned a personal computer or had access at work. By the year 2000, American On Line, by itself, was claiming to have 135 million individual e-mail addresses!

The Web allows a campaign to dispense information at unbelievably low cost. Bare in mind the obvious, that people need computers to tap into the Internet to access the Web. Nevertheless, the information dispensing possibilities for campaigns are monumental.

Position Papers

For campaigns, which continue to believe that issues and position papers are important, the information can be put on the Web. [See the appendix, here, for a partial list of the huge number of organizations and politicians that have been using the Web, just since 1995.]

A campaign can put its positions on issues into a brochure type of presentation on the Web and save the expense of mailing out printed pieces. Also, when a particular group is targeted for support, (a group which is likely to have computers) the benefits can be seen.

Mailings

Consider a candidate running against an incumbent who is perceived to be antibusiness in a congressional race. The possibilities become limitless for fund raising appeals to be appended to a presentation showing antibusiness votes of the incumbent.

The answer to the question of "how to communicate to a given audience" that a "Web presentation exists" is actually the old fashioned way. Consider a candidate who had the business directories of the local chambers of commerce in the cities that make up a congressional district. Instead of mailing a letter inside an envelope, or a brochure made for the presentation, a postcard could be sent. The message on the postcard could read something like:

"Dear Smithville Business Leader: Do you realize just HOW *antibusiness* our representative in Congress is? On the Internet, (the Web), check out the votes our congressman has on taxes, foreign trade, and depreciation schedules. Dial up http://**www.jonesforcongress.com** . You won't believe it until you've seen it!"

In the Web presentation, the votes of the congressman, explanations of the votes, and an appeal for support and fundraising can all be done.

Then, consider the benefits of using a postcard vis a vis mailing a letter or brochure. First, many envelopes never get opened. A postcard with the "URL" (URL is "uniform resource locator" which in normal English means a "Web address") highlighted, as in the example above, is seen as soon as the postcard is looked at. Second, whereas a letter or brochure may not get read, even if opened, anyone who dials up a Web URL is actually doing so to read it. Further, a postcard can be set aside to be referenced at a later, more convenient time from when the mailing is received. A letter or brochure is usually just discarded, if it is inconvenient for the receiver to peruse at the moment. Also, none of this addresses the "time difference." Web presentation pages are "up there" 24 hours a day, for as long as the campaign desires, and can be modified. A mailing is here today and gone the next.

Business Cards

The flexibility of a Web presentation is another feature. Consider a candidate who gives a talk to a local service club: a Rotary, Lions, Kiwanis, 20–30 Club, etc. Even in a situation where it might be considered crass to pass out campaign brochures and literature, it is nevertheless usually permissible to pass out business cards. Consider passing out business cards with a Web URL included in addition to the usual information—along with a teaser sentence. This can be referenced during a speech: "I don't have time here to tell you of all the antibusiness votes of my opposition—but check out my Internet Web pages—and you can see all the details to back up what I've said here today. My Internet Web address is on my business card." [Compare this addition of a URL to the use of the "people card" discussion in Chapter 10.]

Also, Web pages can be used in place of a campaign newsletter to keep the faithful aware of what the campaign is doing.

13

The Candidate

Chapter 2, "Campaigns," touched upon some problems confronted by candidates.

Except for those areas where a political machine "places" a candidate into a seat, a candidate is the focus of the campaign. As such, the various pressures both from within and from without the campaign will impact a candidate.

The outline in this manual, which addresses the "proper way" to approach the problem of campaign organization and the methods to use for getting votes, should alleviate many of the standard problems faced by candidates. Most of these problems center on a candidate having the impression that he/she is supposed to be expert at many things in which they have had no practical experience.

Notions

However, there are areas that the candidate can trip over, if he/she is not paying attention. These areas usually center on mistaken notions, which a candidate has built up in mind over what a "candidate" is. This is the old problem of the "magic transformation" of a campaign from out of the realm of the ordinary and into something bigger than life. "It ain't so."

Most candidates tend to become impressed with the fact that they are candidates for a position. That impression is translated into the feeling of acting like a candidate seen on the "6:00 News," whatever that may be. There is a "mythology" which purports to hold that a candidate's views are all of a sudden much more important than they were before the person became a candidate.

These impressions get caught up in the reality that a candidate is not more important, "all of a sudden." Knowledgeable people will judge the candidate in light of how well the campaign is progressing, not how much the candidate knows. Just as in the section in this manual on "issues," the question of "so what?" is the brutal final judgment.

The unavoidable standard, which confronts a candidate, is the ultimate judgment of the voters through the ballot box. This means that the job of the candidate is to get votes, not to make pronouncements on issues, etc.

The inevitable pressures of well wishers must be understood. Just as most people do not understand the job of campaigning, so too, assessments of the campaign by observers must be taken in the light of the observer's knowledge. A well-organized campaign, which is moving forward and making contact with thousands of voters, will not be telegraphing this fact to observers. Yet, a "cocktail party observer," pointing out that he doubts the campaign is going anywhere, because he has seen no newspaper advertisements, can have an effect on a candidate.

Spouses

A candidate's family must be taken into account. At a minimum, the tacit support of the spouse is necessary. Also, the spouse should be considered as a receiver of campaign information. A spouse has the first word of the day and the last word of the day with the candidate. All the good works, of campaign workers and strategists along the lines set forth here, can be seriously undermined by a spouse who continues to propound a conflicting concept to the candidate. Just as candidates can have their head "turned" by being put in the spotlight, so too can spouses, who never paid attention to politics previously, but all of a sudden become penetrating political strategists.

In the event the spouse of a candidate is not to be included into the inner campaign workings, for one reason or another, a project should be assigned to the spouse.

The sacrifices in time and familial support, among other areas, by the spouse, during the course of the campaign and the activities of the candidate, do in fact call for consideration and understanding by the campaign for the spouse. Hopefully, a campaign will not be sidetracked by a spouse. Also, the spouse need not be a decision-maker in the campaign, but certainly, the goodwill of the spouse is obviously necessary and appropriate.

A Proprietary Campaign

In the early stages of a campaign, candidates often get caught in a dilemma over how much to disclose about the campaign. A well-meaning person will approach the candidate to ask how the campaign is doing. Many times the object of the query is to see if help could be used, if offered. However, a candidate will mistake the question for one seeking out how the campaign is progressing. The answer of the candidate is often much along the lines that "the campaign is coming along quite well, thank you. It has several projects, which it is pressing forward with. Also, there are many very good people working on the campaign, etc."

The impression left on the person who asked the question is that in fact things are moving along swimmingly, and that no more help is needed by the campaign. What the reality of the situation may be is most often all together different. What the candidate meant, in his answer to the question of the campaign's progress, was that they had been working on sketching out some projects, that there were some good people who have indicated they MAY be able to help out, and that the campaign will probably be moving forward at some point in the future.

What was a potential offer of help, got dropped because the questioner could see no room to make an offer of help. Especially, since everything came over so good, anyway.

It should be standard procedure for a candidate to ask an interested person if they would be willing to help the campaign. With the procedures outlined in this manual, there should be a place for anyone who says they could help. The help can be in the voter side of the campaign, the public side, the inventorying side, or the influence side. If the candidate has organized the campaign with areas of responsibility for each member of the kitchen cabinet, the coordinator/manager and project heads, there should always be someone who is in a position to factor in some new help. Knowing this, a candidate can say that Mrs. Smith "will be calling" to the potential helper.

It is the candidate, after all, who is the focus of the work of the campaign. While there are many people who "altruistically" will work for "the good of the 10th district," or the party, most people consider themselves to be working for "John." The candidate is also the person with the most forceful request for help in his/her campaign.

Drawing Opposition Blood

Many idealistic candidates do not understand the nature of the opposition and consider the election race "just" an exercise in democracy. This is where a good campaign is run and the best campaign wins. These candidates know that nasty things have happened in campaigns, and chances are they have heard of some potential "dirt" about the opposition, but the ideal is always there. Consequently, when the campaign starts to heat up, the candidate is not prepared for it.

A campaign can often start to heat up with attacks, innuendo, and slanted reporting by the media. A good gauge of a campaign's progress is the intensity of the opposition to it. The nastier the letters to the editor, the better! The more vicious the rumors about the candidate or their spouse, the better! These attacks should be understood for what they represent and should not be feared. No one likes this fact, but it is merely a milepost on the path to doing the job in the position the candidate is running for.

As the positive progress of a candidate's campaign becomes apparent to the opposition, especially an incumbent, a bitterness will sweep over them. Real money, power and influence are not lightly given up.

A good example of "drawing opposition blood" and the various reactions to it was seen in a congressional race some years ago. It was early in the race. The incumbent Democrat Congressman had made an expensive survey quite early and was pleased with the results, but he was uncertain of the coming intensity of the conservative Republican's campaign. By and large, as the Republican made charges against the Democrat in newsreleases, the charges were answered by the local large daily newspapers through their political reporters.

The Republican ran an advertisement in the paper, which accused the Congressman of straddling the busing issue, which was hot at the time. Each straddle of being on both sides of the issue was documented in the ad under a "look for yourself" section.

The result of the ad was a furious editorial by the newspaper "answering" the ad, charge by charge. The editorial went on to accuse the Republican of all sorts of transgressions.

The effect on the Republican was devastating. How could he be accused of doing such things, publicly? His reaction was to try to right the wrongs that the editorial had pointed out even to the point or restructuring his campaign organization. This included eliminating some of the people who had advised using the advertisement seen in the paper.

The reaction was the reverse of what it should have been. Such a long editorial in the newspaper, which was an enemy of the Republican, should have been welcomed as a sign that the campaign was being taken seriously. The candidate never understood the logic of the situation. To the degree that the newspaper, which was clearly on the incumbent's side, would applaud any actions by the Republican, that would be the degree to suspect that things were not going well for the campaign.

In a situation where the campaign of a challenger is the brunt of derogatory information or actions, especially by the media, the actions should not be answered. As mentioned above, the worse the allegations, the more progress the campaign is making. Should the candidate be questioned about the dirt thrown at him by the newspaper, he should shrug it off. It would be like trying to prove a negative. It can't be done.

Keeping Focus

Everyone has his or her own personality. Yet, in some cases people have gotten to a position in spite of their personality.

A person who is a candidate certainly got to that point with all the baggage of their personality, for better or for worse. However, they are not incumbents until elected. Unfortunately, some candidates, unbeknownst to themselves, put people off with what are considered affectations.

Rightly or wrongly, too strong an emphasis on a personality feature can be considered to be affected. A devout man can sometimes let his piety become a hindrance. The same holds for one who abstains from alcohol. Extremes of sincerity can come over to other people in a reverse manner.

Basically, people are considering a candidate for a political position. Anything non-germane to that will only get in the way. If possible, a candidate needs to be reminded to not force a package deal on the voters. They may want the politics, but they may not swallow the piety. The difference in the reaction of an influential potential supporter can be considerable in the form of monetary support. While no campaign worker could ever get away with approaching a candidate about "wearing his piety on his sleeve," there remains the route of playing "devil's advocate." "How will this be perceived." is a useful question, should the need arise.

Public Speaking

Quite often a candidate is not an accomplished public speaker. This can impact him or her from two sides. First, there is the obvious problem of the need to make a good presentation. However the second, is often less understood in the beginning. It is the problem of having good material in a speech.

A person not familiar with making public presentations will not have the experience of knowing the ingredients of holding the attention of an audience. Also, the novice in speaking will usually be too busy trying to remember what to say, reading notes, or worrying about what to do with his/her hands, than to try to sense the receptive mood of the audience. Some preparatory homework can take the edge off of these problems.

The first basic fundamental of talking to any group is to know what that group is interested in. If the candidate talks about something else, the candidate wastes everyone's time, including his own. Even a presidential candidate, Barry Goldwater in 1964, could not break such a rule. He spoke on crime in St. Petersburg, Florida, where the retired people who came to hear him speak, wanted to hear his views on Social Security. The *St. Petersburg Times* even headlined, "Right city, wrong speech." Then, in poverty stricken West Virginia, Goldwater hit President Johnson's antipoverty program.[73] Goldwater did not have to promise more handouts to the audience. However, certain realities are too strong to buck. At worst, he should have avoided an area, if he could not speak to a local audience about local interests.

After knowing what a group is interested in, a speaker should have a beginning and also an end for the talk. In the beginning, the triteness of telling an old joke, is too obvious. However, the beginning of any talk MUST answer the "so what?" question. Simply telling why the talk is important to the listeners is all that is necessary. It clarifies the matter for both a speaker and the listeners.

The ending of the talk is the most important part of the exercise, because the speaker can get in a last call for action. An ending should be considered as the final "pitch." Remembering that the campaign wants votes or help, the ending of a talk should be structured so as to allow people to approach the candidate after the talk, to volunteer help. The ending of the talk provides this transition. In this way a listener can come up afterward and say that in light of the speaker's last comment, "Here I am." A speaker, who does not have this part of the speech well planned, loses the whole reason for the talk. To reiterate, education and advocacy are not the objects of a talk. The only reason why any candidate should take the time to give a talk is when something positive and tangible for the campaign will come out of it.

The body of the talk is the substance of the presentation. Issues arising out of a district inventory and with people of influence will be the best sources of material for the talk, so long as they are relevant to the object (audience and subject) at hand. The goal should be to get as close to the listeners on their interest level as possible with material in the talk. However, there is a problem many candidates do not understand, and the problem comes from overestimating their status as a candidate. If the credentials of the candidate do not include obvious "credibility factors" for the subject being spoken on, the candidate must establish his own credibility by using references to authority.

This is to say that a professional musician, as a candidate, has very little credibility in diagnosing a problem such as inflation for an audience. Even when the credibility problem has been recognized, often the "remedy" has been the timewasting search for authoritative references in various literature. This is often the process of searching for quotations by spokesmen from the conservative point of view.

One answer to the problem of authority, is to use headlines

from newspapers or especially, magazines. Most libraries of any size at all have a file of *U.S. News & World Report*. Merely scanning the headlines of several issues can quite often find a headline, which states the case for something the candidate wants to talk about. There is a huge difference for a speech maker in saying, "Medicare will go broke in 20 years, unless its costs are cut," "according to an article in *U.S. News & World Report* magazine, versus, trying to drag out the numbers of billions spent on physicians versus prescriptions, versus home care, and so forth.

A word to the wise, here. Candidates can get tripped up, just after they have alleged something, by being asked (especially by a newspaper reporter) to "name one local example." In not being able to name a specific, particular example, candidates can be damaged, publicly. Again, this can be handled by pointing out a headline of an article that named many examples. One example of this was when, after a speech, a candidate was asked about his allegations of welfare fraud in the area. (Of course this violates the ideas put forth in this manual on what "issues" to use.) The candidate was asked to name one example in the area. He couldn't, and it was remarked upon in several newspapers. Had he referenced an article headline, he could have pointed out that there was a whole article on the problem in the XYZ magazine, showing how prevalent the problem was. He could, then, have mentioned the approximate size of the local county welfare budget, or, alluded to the fact, that, with welfare spending at so many millions of dollars annually, the potential for fraud was too great for anyone to say it was not present.

Using magazine headlines will shorten the research time necessary for putting together a talk for a group, also. However, the standard amount of time that a new speech requires in the research and writing is about one hour of work for one minute's worth of presentation. This is a Toastmaster's International guideline for the research/compilation ratio to actual presentation. Of course, a candidate will have generated many hours in the course of a campaign gathering material for talks, so that each and every speech does not call for the "one hour–one minute" time investment. However, and obviously, this does not address those who choose to "wing it." But, like anything else, "they get what they pay for." This means results out of a speech will follow effort put into the talk.

What cannot be avoided, however, is the necessity for preparation for a *good* talk. The reason speeches are given is to persuade listeners to take some form of action for the campaign. To persuade people to take action calls for a good presentation by the speaker, or at least, a compelling presentation. If the candidate cannot envision positive results from making a presentation, such a presentation is not worth the time for travel and delivery. The mere residual effect of possibly "showing the colors" or "raising name identification" by spending several hours of waiting at an event, and commuting to an event, is a major waste of time.

Yet, it is very difficult to turn down a requested appearance. However, a campaign must make the determination that there is something to be gained from a presentation. A calculation should consider how close to the defined direction of the campaign any appearance would be. This is to say, based upon a campaign outline discussed in kitchen cabinet meetings for a whole campaign, is any given appearance consistent with the goals previously discussed?

It is ego gratifying to make a presentation to a group. It is also ego gratifying to have some people come up to the candidate after a presentation to compliment him or her on the talk. However, a campaign calculus must consider the possibility of, 1. getting one or two possible volunteers from the expenditure of a whole evening by the candidate at a meeting, versus, 2. more efficiently spending time planning how to find more influential people to contact. Every action a campaign takes must be calculated in the "time versus votes" trade off. Personal appearances and talks by the candidate are some of the hardest on which to work the calculus.

There is an easy rapid-fire test to apply for making a decision as to whether or not to make an appearance. After looking at the above factors and deciding the interest area of the audience and the relevant issue to use with the audience, a candidate and the kitchen cabinet may apply a "relaxation test." In the last analysis, the candidate must be relaxed in the use of this material and he must be relaxed in the appearance before the group. If either of these "relaxation tests" are violated, the chances of the appearance generating positive results in votes or volunteers for the campaign are greatly diminished.

The test effectively precludes speaking in front of a hostile audience, everything else being equal. If the goal of an appearance is to get something for the campaign, the mere courage used in making such an appearance is a waste. Unless courage can be translated into positive, results producing factors, it is a waste of time. There are too many neutral people who can be contacted through other means, which could produce votes for a campaign, to waste resources through some sort of misguided "political evangelism."

Arguing

It should go without saying that arguing about issues by the candidate in a public setting is thoroughly counterproductive. Unfortunately, in the midst of discussing politically charged issues, disagreements can lead to heated tempers.

There is an axiom about arguing that a candidate is well advised to remember. Raised voices and blood pressure are "equal" in the energy expended between two people in a disagreement. Two or more yelling people caustically disagreeing with one another are all equal, as is what they are "defending." This is in the eyes of the people who may be watching the confrontation. No facts or figures are relevant in a heated argument. The only relevant factor in arguing is the fact that emotions have overtaken both sides. In such a case, both candidates

L

automatically lose. This is because either one's facts and figures become "leveled" with those of the person being argued
with.

Should a candidate get into a public disagreement, which
becomes argumentative, he or she must immediately step above
the argument. This is done by dissolving the focus on the other
person or persons, which are causing the disagreement. (Observe two arguing people. They become highly intent on each
other. The battle is very personal.) Calmly and with comments to
the effect of "give me a phone call later and we'll continue the
discussion" should shed the argument. If an arguer persists, the
candidate could force the problem by appealing to the listeners
as to whether they want to waste more time listening to an argument. If even that does not work (as for instance, being on a
stage in front of an audience sensing the possibility of a "battle")
the candidate should focus on the opposition person's raised voice,
blood pressure, or red face. Calm, relaxed comments and slow
deep breathing in the face of the storm should disarm it. And,
moving onto the next subject with all due speed, will help, also.

Debates

Many candidates envision themselves as fully able to compete, and if not necessarily totally able to devastate an adversary,
to at least overwhelm the foe. As it was pointed out in the chapter
on issues, debates are approached in different ways by different
campaigns and personalities.

Unless there are considerable reasons for a debate, the
amount of time put into debate preparation can be better used
elsewhere. However, in the event a campaign decides that a given
debate will be in its best interests, the following observations
may help.

It is a rare political debate where both sides confront the
given "topic" of a debate with an eye toward providing an honest
airing of the differences between opposing camps or viewpoints.

Furthermore, even when both sides begin in such a manner, the realities of a debate format and a live audience can often change the initial objectives of the debaters.

A basic reality of a debate is that time constraints turn legitimate discussion of points into some form of sloganeering. It was mentioned, earlier, that there is not enough time (no matter what the format) to develop one issue, let alone several issues. One further example in the present context illustrates the problem of "so little time."

The March, 1978, issue of *Reason* magazine, carried an extraordinarily well done article called, "Billion Dollar bumpers." The article was about 5,000 words long. The subtitle of the article was, "They are merely 'safety' bumpers, they say, but these cumbersome, weighty items, not only contribute nothing to safety, but in some way affect every facet of vehicle performance." The article was concise and tightly written; it was distilled from a book by the author, Jack Solomon. The book was called, *The Billion-Dollar Bumper Bust.* In a fact-filled presentation, the author traced the conception of the legislation behind the creation of the monster bumpers on cars in the '70's. He traced the implementation of the legislation, and its effects. Then, he proved that the results of the act and the actualization of having the bumpers on autos created the exact reverse of what was intended. It was shown that cars became heavier, less maneuverable, less safe, and less energy efficient than they would have been otherwise without the monster bumpers.

If a tightly written magazine article on automobile bumpers needs 5,000 words, cogently, to put forth a position, consider the magnitude of a subject such as national defense, energy policy, social security or Medicare. A debate on auto bumpers, which was able to shed any light on the subject, would be long and tedious. A debate on a broad issue is really futile.

The basic problem in a debate becomes one of definition. Each side will define the issue of the debate in its own interests. A debater must define the issue in his best interests. He should define what is at issue and why it is at issue. Further, he should also define the time frame involved and the geography. After this, the best arguments of the opposition must be considered, before the debate, in order to find the best counter arguments. Finally, liberals/statists invariably solve problems in society with force, i.e., a law. A conservative would be well advised to find and understand the coercive basis of a probable hidden argument that the opposition (statist) will make. In this manner of defining an issue, a legitimate debate on the merits of an issue can be attempted.

However, there is a second round of preparation for a debate, which needs to be made. This second round should be made to combat the effects of those seen in the sample debate in this manual in the chapter on issues. The second round of preparation is for when the opposition retreats into tag lines. Therefore, a candidate should have his own bag of goodies for doing battle on a tag line basis.

When a debate degenerates into tag lines, it has changed into a battle of theatrics. A debater should be prepared with slogans and personality tags to confront the thrust of the other side. "Teddy, 'Do as I say,' not as I do, Kennedy." Or, "That sounds like 'Hairdo a Week, Hillary." (When pointing to flip flops.) Tying a distasteful attribute from a well-known personality onto the arguments of the opposition debater is unsettling to him. However, a word to the wise is necessary. The candidate who would use such an artifice, needs to have prepared to do it, usually with a small group of close supporters, which has discussed its implementation. They would set the stage, set the likely scenario, and only then, use a preselected line. For those who are squeamish about using such tactics, it need only be pointed out that the opposition can do it "naturally." Should a legitimate candidate not be prepared?

The above preparation is for an event that hopefully could be sidestepped! A debate, which moves into tag lines, will leave an audience polarized. Nothing is likely to be gained, certainly no votes or volunteers for the campaign. Saving a "psychological round" with tag lines, preselected, is small consolation for wasting so much time, however.

A more effective crowd pleaser in a debate situation is to use the concept of "political cross dressing," so named by Michael Emerling in a December 1977 article in *Reason* magazine. The essence of the concept is to use the adjectives of the opposition in support of your own side. Emerling quoted Milton Friedman from a February 1973 interview in magazine as a very good example of the technique. Friedman said: "You very seldom find poor people testifying in favor of the minimum wage. The people who do are those who receive or pay wages much higher than the minimum." Environmentalists can be debated by using the idea of "quality of life" against them, when talking about building new roads, etc. The "right to privacy" can be used effectively against liberal defenders of omnipotent government and its bureaucrats and the laws that set them into power. "Freedom of choice" can be used in many contexts.

Another almost perfect rejoinder to liberals, advocating another stupid proposal, is to point out the number of jobs that could be lost. "How many spotted owls are worth the wasted working lives of logging men on welfare?" "How many hours out of a person's life are worth a 'wetland's policy' where highways cannot be built—but which would save lives and hours of commuting?"

However in all cases, a candidate must not lose sight of the reason for an appearance. A candidate is in a debate to find votes or support (not to educate on an issue). An audience needs to be the focus of the debater—either the audience in attendance or the media audience, which will read reports on the debate in the local media. Richard Nixon found this out when debating JFK. Kennedy was talking to the TV audience in the famous first 1960 debate. Nixon was talking to Kennedy in that debate, about the "issues." Kennedy got what he was there for. That Kennedy was there for the theatrics was given away in the media reports, sometime later, as to the debate in his inner circle about the color of suit to wear. Kennedy's dark blue suit stole the platform from Nixon in his light gray suit, before Nixon said his first word. "Form," not substance, told the tale to a very large degree.

In view of all the variables, a campaign really needs to ask itself if it can't just plead "too busy a schedule," when a debate offer comes to the campaign.

14

Citizens Groups

This manual has been designed as a discussion of various methods and ideas for electioneering for candidates. There is an adjunct to the process, which can be extremely valuable, if used properly. This adjunct is a citizens group, which has been formed especially to endorse candidates.

Such citizens groups are usually ad hoc committees of politically and community concerned people. The group is often called, Citizens for Good Government, or Concerned Citizens of Oakville, or something similarly non-partisan. The group will tend to support sound, rather conservative, community-minded candidates. The support for candidates from the group is usually in the form of an endorsement and sometimes, modest monetary contributions. Oftentimes the group will take out its own advertisements in newspapers. The utility of such support is that a group represents visible, solid community-grounded interest in a candidate.

Characteristics of these citizens groups are often two-fold (among others). First, the group will likely have several professionals and other prominent people in the community. The second is that the group is quite often extremely limited in the actions it can take, because the principals simply do not have time out of their busy schedule. This is important, because in some cases these groups can be called "do nothing." This is extremely unfortunate and indicates ignorance on the part of those who "point the finger."

However, the lack of time for action leads the groups, most often, to have a limited number of meetings, usually monthly, and often with a summer break. Also, one or two activists tend to do most of the work of keeping the group together.

Another problem endemic to groups of this sort, is that keeping focused on an issue/candidate, is a chore. Often the group cannot decide on what the "best" method or avenue of political action is (or should be . . .). Discussions often bog down on some particular gnawing, but not exciting, issue in the area. Or, many in attendance will agree that, "Brown is doing a lousy job as a politician to represent the area," but then the group disagrees as to how to go about replacing him. After a lunch meeting (or whatever) is over, no course of action will have been decided upon.

In many cases, discussions within a group as noted above will bog down over the question of which comes first, the candidate or the issue. This is in the context of elected officials in areas from city council to Congress. The discussions will take many turns but will end up in disagreement over the "which comes first" question.

The following suggestions should overcome the problem of the dilemma above, and should also help a candidate who does receive an endorsement from a citizen's group. A group must focus on a particular office it wishes to change. This is most often the office, which has the worst incumbent, but may be a lesser office if the worst is somehow intimidating.

Once a representative office, which is to be the object of attention, has been chosen, the matter becomes one of finding a candidate to replace the incumbent. The problem of "issues" must be squashed along the lines covered here.

Finding candidates can be difficult, but there are established lines for a search. Finding a current office holder, in a lesser position than the office being considered, who is willing to make the race, is best, e.g., a city councilman for a county supervisor's seat. This is, if the office holder meets the requirements as pro-pounded and sought-after by the group. If there are no current incumbents available, former office holders or former candidates provide further areas for consideration. Beyond that, party leaders in the area may know of attractive possibilities who have been active in party or community affairs but who have just not been "tapped" previously. Another step is to consider the leadership of various community organizations and service clubs in the area, the chamber of commerce, Rotary, Kiwanis, Lions or Soroptimists, PTA's, etc.

Once some potential candidates are found, some background material may be of help to let the group know about the individual. A low key approach can then be made to the person or persons—along the lines that support may be available for the right person, would they be interested in talking? The group can then decide how it will make a formal decision whether to support the individual. The group should be fairly certain of its choice before it actually makes the approach to the potential candidate, however.

It can be seen that it will take some time to run through a checklist, searching out candidates from political offices, and, or groups. However, it is just this sort of activity which a group should undertake, rather than debating what to do or what direction to take. One person with a checklist made from the foregoing points can give the group guidance.

Once a candidate is found, the standard types of support can be extended at the proper time. However, the best possible support that such a group could offer any candidate is the support of being a "master influence group." The great impact this can have can be understood from the chapter here on a district inventory.

Each member of a citizen's group, who is in the position of having some influence in the community and who knows other such people, should introduce the candidate to several influential people through the lunch meeting device. This would be an

L

invaluable catapult for the candidate. It is also a form of support, which only a citizens group can bestow to a significant degree.

Another invaluable service a citizens group could do for the candidate is to meet with the candidate in a "working lunch" setting where the group runs through a district inventory of influential people in the important areas in the district. Much of the hard research of the campaign could be completed in such a session by actually having the influential people point out who the others are and how to approach them!

Another area in which a citizens group might be able to help is the area of little known political offices. While the group can focus on a particularly bad politician, who needs to be ousted, the group can also put some of its own sponsored people into obscure positions. This builds a fund of talent for later years.

In the *Los Angeles Times*, during the 1994 campaign, there was an article which disclosed that some minorities in certain areas were focusing on some water district's elected boards of directors. The paper indicated that the minorities had discovered that there were lucrative service supply contracts let out by sanitation, water, and other special representative boards. The way certain organized minority groups went after the seats on the boards (which not one in ten voters really *knew* about) was to form an organization with a similar name to the board in question. "The Water Conservation Committee" would be set up, a likely candidate for the upcoming election would get a seat with the "Committee's" board, and then list that position on the ballot as a name identifier. Therefore, in an election for the South Basin Municipal Water District, there would be a candidate running whose "occupation" was listed as "Board Member, Water Conservation Committee." It was working in the areas the *Times* was covering.

Quite often, political parties have done the same sort of thing. However, quite often, the old "machine" in an area has lost its wider, "peripheral," view.

The simplest way for a group to find out what obscure elected board positions may be available, is to check the last several election cycles at a city clerk's office (or other municipal/county office which is in charge of elections for the area). It is surprising to many people, the number of elected boards which are largely disregarded by the voters at large. These positions can be explored further. Quite often, the incumbent board members were appointed years earlier, and have been re-elected handily ever since.

In short, with no more meetings than a citizens group is used to, it can nevertheless become a force to be reckoned with. Having a goal, and the direction to get to the goal, is the larger part of what is needed.

15

A Final Word: Tying It All Together

The suggestions presented in this work have been presented in a positive light. The suggestions have been designed to get a campaign on the right track from the beginning, so that as little time as possible will be lost groping for a direction.

The various elements presented can lead to victory for a campaign, which will plan its moves, organize the effort, and follow through with action. The items, which have been suggested for particular implementation, have been selected to give the greatest impact for the smallest investment.

The three fronts of a campaign have been designed to be mutually reinforcing. A campaign to court influential people will spill over into influencing many average voters. A postcard campaign (asking for the votes) and a sign campaign will reinforce each other and the influential people.

Each of the three campaigns will be independently reinforcing within themselves. A campaign organization will be reinforced in its efforts by seeing the signs out and seeing the piles of postcards build up. The search and courting of influential people will reinforce itself through the fundraising process. The whole campaign effort will gain a symmetry of action, which from the point of view of the impact on the opposition, will become almost kaleidoscopic.

There will be criticism of the campaign approach suggested here. One of the first will be that the campaign is simplistic, especially in the belief that an incumbent congressman could be beaten with postcards. The answer, which was given in the text, more than covers this objection. There is no more inexpensive, less intrusive, nor more personal way to "get to," or communicate with, the average voter, who doesn't care deeply about the election, than with personally written and addressed postcards.

Another criticism is that the campaign is cold and uses people. The reverse is actually the case. What could be colder than spending vast quantities of dollars in a big media campaign with lots of computerized direct mail and blaring radio and TV spots?

A campaign, which seeks out people, is actually the most responsive type of campaign that could be run. Furthermore, in the approach to the various groups of people throughout the district, this type of campaign benefits *real* candidates.

Perhaps the best thing about the approach in this work is that it will be totally unexpected by an opposition. Different authorities on the political might of incumbent congressmen estimate the clout of incumbency at from $500,000 to $1.5 million. The clout of state legislators is proportionately considerable, as it is with school board members and city council people, etc. Incumbents will put out effort, but they will feel secure in their re-election efforts.

The planning and the efforts in the approach suggested in this work will only become apparent to the opposition once the full force of the efforts become apparent. By then, it will be too late to counter the efforts with like efforts. If the first round of postcards hits in late September, the second round should hit in mid-October. The one-day finance plan would take place shortly after the first round of postcards hit. Sniping signs will have already had their locations mapped out for posting once they are made, shortly after the one-day finance committee. The signs will go up at the end of September. Save the lawn sign blitz for the last week of October. All the while, the courting of influential people has been going on for months.

By the time the second round of postcards hits the district, the campaign can be assured that there will be considerable notice on the part of the media that "something is going on." The same notice will take hold on the part of the opposition. However, by the middle of October, the best that can be done by way of countering these efforts is to purchase electronic media when the desirable times have largely been committed to commercial accounts. Should a campaign have more resources, the media it can afford should be used in the last couple of weeks of October, even when it has been purchased substantially earlier.

Throughout the whole campaign, the opposition will be powerless to counter what it "feels" happening because no "issues" will have been used. The only counter is saturation media/mail. Yet, the voter in the face of a saturation media by the opposition will get a final personal request for his/her vote from the final postcard, mailed five or six days before the election.

There is no use for some sort of "issue" blunderbuss in this scenario. It is the embodiment of what B.H. Liddell Hart calls the "indirect approach." In his book, *Strategy*, he says, " . . . effective results in war have rarely been attained unless the approach has had such indirectness as to ensure the opponent's unreadiness to meet it."[74]

Remember, an incumbent will know that the leadership of the opposition party has not targeted the district. There is a smugness about such knowledge that will work very well for the program outlined here. The same holds for the "heir apparent" in a "safe" district.

This, then, is the way for conservatives in low budget campaigns to oust those who don't really "represent" the views held by the people in a district.

"Fools say that they learn by experience. I prefer to profit by others' experience." (Bismarck)

Finally, then, the day after the election, a winning conservative can realize that deep felt yearning in his/her heart. The day after the election, a conservative can talk about "issues." The day after the election, as a winner, his/her views will in fact be important!

16

References and Notes

[1] *Greensboro Daily News*, Nov. 7, 1974 p. B1

[2] Ibid., Nov. 11, 1974

[3] Murray Rothbard, *America's Great Depression*, Nash Publishing, Los Angeles, p. 16

[4] Peter Wychoff, *Psychology of Stock Market Timing*, Prentice-Hall, Inc., New Jersey, 1963

[5] Harry D. Schultz, *Financial Tactics and Terms for the Sophisticated International Investor*, Harper & Row, New York, 1974, p. 56

[6] *San Francisco Sunday Chronicle & Examiner*: April 30, 1978, "Managers Must Have Free Trade in Ideas."

[7] *Viewpoint*, Stockton, CA, March 1978

[8] *Wall Street Journal*, May 25, 1977

[9] *Human Events*, April 6, 1974

[10] Ibid., June 28, 1975

[11] *Success Unlimited*, October 1977

[12] *Reason* magazine, January 1978

[13] *U.S. News & World Report*, Jan. 31, 1977

[14] *Success Unlimited*, October 1977

[15] Theodore H. White, *Making of the President 1964*, Signet Books, New York, 1966, p. 379

[16] *San Francisco Chronicle*, Sept. 27, 1975, p.6

[17] Ibid.

[18] *Almanac of American Politics*, 1978, p. 820.

[19] *Human Events*, May 28, 1977 p. 1

[20] *Wall Street Journal*, Aug. 27, 1970, "Cloudy Crystal Ball."

[21] Ibid., March 23, 1972, "A Modern Machine"

[22] *Almanac of American Politics*, 1978, p. 821

[23] *Almanac*, Op. Cit., p. 633

[24] *The Commonwealth*, Jan. 2, 1978

[25] *San Francisco Chronicle*, July 7, 1975

[26] *Human Events*, April 1, 1978, "Conservative Forum."

[27] Robert Agranoff, *Management of Election Campaigns* Holbrook Press, *Inc.*, Boston, 1976, p. XiV.

[28] Stephen C. Shadegg, *How to Win an Election*, Crestwood Books, Arlington, VA, 1968, p. 50

[29] Napolean Hill, *Think & Grow Rich*

[30] Hal Evry, *The Selling of a Candidate*, Western Opinion Research Center, Los Angeles, 1971

[31] Wm. L. Riordan, *Plunkitt of Tammany Hall*, E.P.Dutton & Co., N.Y. 1963, p. 26

[32] Robert Agranoff, Op. Cit., p. 285

[33] Hal Evry, Op. Cit., p. 60

[34] *Advertising Age*, March 20, 1978, "Garth Looks Beyond Political Arenas."

[35] Shadegg, Op. Cit., p. 17

[36] Shadegg, Op. Cit., p. 194

[37] *Greensboro Daily News*, Nov 4, 1974

[38] *Kasten Plan*, Committee for the Survival of a Free Congress

[39] *San Francisco Examiner*, Aug. 8, 1976,"Carter Team in Trouble on Donations."

[40] *Success Unlimited*, November 1976, p. 76

[41] *Oakland Tribune*, Feb. 8, 1976, "Breck Seeks Dellums Seat."

[42] *Viewpoint*, March 1978, "Norm Shumway Launches Door to Door Campaign for Congress."

[43] undated, "Harmer for Senate," brochure, 1976, California

[44] *Oakland Tribune*, Nov. 1, 1974

[45] *Hayward Daily Review*, Oct. 15, 1976
[46] *Greensboro Daily News*, Nov. 1, 1974, "Rep. Preyer Rebuts Charge that He's a Big Spender."
[47] *Hayward Daily Review*, Oct. 24, 1974, "Stark Says Inflation Cure Must be Something Radical."
[48] *California Business*, May 8, 1975
[49] *Wall Street Journal*, Sept. 25, 1975
[50] *Wall Street Journal*, April 2, 1975
[51] *California Business*, March 16, 1978
[52] November 19, 1975
[53] *U.S. News & World Report*, April 17, 1978
[54] *Wall Street Journal*, Feb. 8, 1978
[55] *Hayward Daily Review*, Dec. 27, 1977, "ABAG Directory Helps Cut Red Tape."
[56] *Hayward Daily Review*, Aug. 31, 1975, "Where Does the Tax Money Go?"
[57] *Libertarian Party News*, March-April 1976
[58] Edward Gobbon, *Decline & Fall of the Roman Empire*, Vol III, p. 177, Everyman's Library Edition, E.P. Dutton, New York
[59] Gibbon, Op.Cit., p. 118
[60] Gibbon, Op.Cit., p.178
[61] Gibbon, Op.Cit., Vol. IV, p. 357
[62] Gibbon, Op.Cit, Vol. IV
[63] *San Francisco Sunday Examiner & Chronicle*, March 26, 1978, "The New Political Clout of Industry."
[64] *Hayward Daily Review*, Oct. 5, 1976, editorial
[65] *Hayward Daily Review*, Feb. 6, 1977, "Week in Review."
[66] *Advertising Age*, Mar. 20, 1978, "Garth . . ."
[67] *Wall Street Journal*, June 1, 1978, "Politics & People."
[68] *Hayward Daily Review*, Oct. 5, 1976, editorial
[69] Agranoff, Op.Cit., p. 255
[70] Shadegg, Op.Cit., p. 198
[71] *Time*, March 7, 1977, "God & Man in Bloomington."
[72] *International Harry Schultz Letter*, HSL #334, P.O.Box 2523, Lausanne 1002, Switzerland

[73] Theodore H. White, *Making of the President 1964*, p. 398.

[74] B.H. Liddell Hart, *Strategy*, Frederick A. Praeger, New York, 1965, p. 25

[75] *L.A. Times*, 11–8–96, page D4

[76] L.A. Times, 11–21–96, page D1

[77] L.A. Times, 12–27–95, page D1

Appendix I

"Special Interest" Absentee Vote Campaign

For "smaller vote" races, non-partisan and others

Goal: 1000 absentee votes
   14 week plan, from July 30 to the first week of November

   = 71 votes per four nights/available to work per week
      [Monday, Tuesday, Wednesday, Thursday]
   = 18 committed votes per night, every night

Source: based on 14,000 potential voting citizens in the community/district of which, based on U.S. demographics, roughly 3% should be in the following categories:

blind	420
deaf	420
disabled/wheel chair	420
shut-ins	420
others/seniors	*420*
Total:	2,100

Other possibilities include various ethnic categories

Goal: to get unregistered voters to register and vote by absentee ballot

Process:

—Get a beginning representative from each group to work with the campaign

—begin recruiting others for the campaign

—start a 3 x 5 card collection (or, computer data base) of people who will commit to vote for the campaign

—done by sending in the voter registration card and then absentee ballot request

—follow-up and hand holding absolutely necessary

The campaign:

—organize volunteers from each group to call friends/find others from the group to tell of the campaign/candidate and the registration and vote request

   —hold weekly meetings for leaders to add up the commitments on 3 x 5 cards [3 x 5 cards with name, address, phone #] "The Smith-for-City-Clerk Club"

      —held at a supporter's home (rotate each week)

      —have cookies, punch—it needs to be **fun** for the workers

         —as a reward for hard work

         —as reinforcement for the workers to meet other workers

  —Weekly number goals for workers recruited

     —for voters committed

     —for getting out (delivering) registration cards (This allows for tracking the needed number goals.)

     —Workers phone their similarly situated friends to ask for a commitment to register and then to vote

—A worker commits to personally deliver the registration requests Follow up phone call thanking the committed voters (to the 3 x 5 cards)

" . . . And we'll check with you when the voter pamphlets come out about sending in the absentee ballot request."

Goal: mid October for sending in all ballot requests [a better alternative: collect SIGNED request forms for ballots and deliver all together to the authorites by the deadline]

The candidate/campaign:

—Will schedule time to go with main recruiters to meet other recruiters and to meet influential voter/opinion leaders of each of the groups

—Will closely track "on schedule" numbers (the goals) of committments coming in (the cumulative 71 per week) (actually more, based on "overage" needed to meet the actual goal

Needs:

—Literature

Minimal: one flyer, photo, three relevant promises/things to do for the given group of voters [business cards could suffice]

—3 x 5 cards: 1,500 at office supply discount store

—a committed project leader and small cadre of workers/phoners/volunteers

Awareness:

—What deadline is for registration

—What deadline is for absentee ballot request

—What deadline is for absentee ballot delivery

Appendix II

Publications Addresses

Business Week
1221 Avenue of the Americas
New York, N.Y. 10020
212–512–2000
Subscriptions:
800–635–1200

The Conservative Action Guide
Human Events
422 First St., SE
Washington, DC 20003

Human Events
422 First St., SE
Washington, DC 20003
202–546–5006
Subscriptions
800–787–7557

The Limbaugh Letter
P.O. Box 420058
Palm Coast, FL 32142–0058
Rush@eibnet.com

Subscriptions:
800–829–5386

U.S. News & World Report
2400 N Street, N.W.,
Washington DC 20037–1196
202–955–2000
Subscriptions:
800–333–8130

[There is no connection between *Campaigning to Win*, nor the author, Gary Bosley, with any of the above publications.]

Tables

Registration, April 1974
Alamance County, North Carolina

Precinct	Dem	Rep	Black	White	Total	Voted May Primary
Albright	522	171	43	699	742	197
C. Boone	1231	384	117	1585	1702	633
N. Boone	1142	446	40	1677	1717	494
S. Boone	1032	364	0	1502	1502	482
W. Boone	267	79	2	365	367	88
E. Burl	1027	246	1	1362	1363	349
N. Burl	1801	187	785	1300	2085	543
S. Burl	1483	301	163	1750	1913	445
W. Burl	1537	255	19	1885	1904	711
Burl 5	1771	670	14	2609	2623	690
Burl 6	1340	285	139	1583	1728	655
Burl 7	1031	188	536	743	1279	312
Coble	701	368	22	1171	1193	281
Faucette	812	218	34	1071	1105	351
S. Graham	1190	359	19	1679	1698	476

W. Graham	543	202	5	814	819	191
E. Graham	1168	314	133	1450	1583	531
N. Graham	982	235	112	1206	1318	403
Graham 3	1443	433	19	2011	2030	567
Haw River	1326	194	422	1190	1612	442
Melville	2317	388	361	2440	2801	901
Morton	912	279	96	1178	1274	341
N. Newlin	514	133	64	603	667	308
S. Newlin	272	151	7	438	445	170
Patterson	448	356	72	808	880	215
Pleasant Grov	886	87	651	358	1009	234
N. Thompson	358	96	92	376	468	160
S. Thompson	535	102	106	554	661	262
Totals	28591	7491	4074	34407	38488	11432

L

Looking for Republican votes:
Low turn-out off-year vs. High turn-out on-year
Alamance County, North Carolina

Precinct	1970 Congressional low-turn-out					1972 Senate high-turn-out				
	rep	dem	total	% Rep	% Dem	Rep	Dem	Total	%Rep	%Dem
Albright	113	141	264	42	53	390	156	546	71	29
W. Boone	43	65	120	35	54	164	109	273	60	40
N. Boone	269	292	589	45	49	761	388	1149	66	34
S. Boone	515	777	1321	38	58	1759	1013	2772	63	37
E. Burl	204	337	600	34	56	826	559	1385	60	40
N. Burl	209	693	941	22	73	601	879	1480	41	59
S. Burl	262	468	763	34	61	887	626	1513	59	41
W. Burl	283	611	915	30	66	716	371	1087	66	34
Burl 5	406	551	990	41	55	1321	689	2010	66	34
Burl6	231	526	765	30	68	722	659	1381	52	48
Burl7	92	291	410	22	70	377	607	984	38	62

Coble	254	161	441	57	36	694	234	928	75	25
Faucette	186	274	502	37	54	550	278	828	66	34
S. Graham	380	517	926	41	56	1256	623	1879	67	33
W. Graham					63	712	537	1249	57	43
E. Graham	239	463	740	32	50	513	277	790	65	35
N. Graham	166	194	388	42	49	1101	524	1625	68	32
Graham 3	322	377	765	42	66	532	526	1058	49	51
Haw River	177	433	657	27						
Melville	311	821	1156	27	71	1081	936	2017	54	46
Morton 218	294	555	39	53	623	348	971	64	36	
N. Newlin	110	180	303	36	59	380	178	558	68	32
S. Newlin	101	95	199	51	48	293	77	370	79	21
Patterson	192	146	361	53	40	499	200	699	71	29
Pleasant Grov	54	340	406	13	84	205	510	715	29	71
N. Thompson	60	185	250	24	74	189	192	381	50	50
S. Thompson	66	202	281	23	72	348	193	541	64	36
Totals	5463	9434	15608	35	60	17498	11689	29187	60	40

*Totals, for vote totals, do not show "other" votes cast for this tabulation. Adding Republican and Democrat votes will not equal "total," because of minor party votes.

Alamance County, North Carolina
A hierarchy of precincts based on Republican greatest potential swing votes from previous elections.
[Analysis is for a race "to be run" in 1974.]

Precinct:	% Change, "base" vote to "enthusiastic" vote
S. Thompson	41
W. Burlington	36
N.Newlin	32
Albright	29
Faucette	29
S. Newlin	28
Melville	27
E. Burlington	26
S. Graham	26
Graham 3	26
West Boone	25
South Boone	25
S. Burlington	25

Burlington 5	25
E. Graham	25
Morton	25
N. Graham	23
Burlington 6	22
North Boone	21
Coble	18
Patterson	18

This listing is based upon the low popularity congressional race Republican percentages in '70 compared to the highly popular senate race Republican percentages of '72. Therefore, the low percentage in the congressional race is subtracted from the high percentage in the senate race. The percentages listed here show the greatest potential percentage swing from a base Republican vote to an "energized" Republican vote. This type of analysis commits the error of using an "on year" Presidential race as compared to an off-year, non-presidential, race. However, by using percentages, it is possible to see where the greatest number of potential "swing" votes are. It would be a waste of time for a Republican candidate to expend resources in precincts not showing on this list.

11-3-1992 Results

For President
A =   Bill Clinton and Al Gore
B =   George Bush and Dan Quayle
C =   Ross Perot and James Stockdale

	A	B	C
ALBRIGHT	279	593	202
CENTRAL BOONE	292	856	190
NORTH BOONE	390	640	173
SOUTH BOONE	424	994	266
WEST BOONE	273	427	141
BOONE 5	359	670	225
EAST BURLINGTON NORTH	316	462	151
BURLINGTON SOUTH	1214	346	118
BURLINGTON	265	225	97
WEST BURLINGTON	426	671	185
BURLINGTON 5	343	677	206
BURLINGTON 6	624	1232	318
BURLINGTON 7	943	353	140
BURLINGTON 8	499	376	135
BURLINGTON 9	431	787	241
COBLE	306	815	236
FAUCETTE	260	593	198
EAST GRAHAM	512	696	204
NORTH GRAHAM	487	409	175
SOUTH GRAHAM	639	1325	387
WEST GRAHAM	215	385	118
GRAHAM 3	575	720	224
HAW RIVER	797	586	215
NORTH MELVILLE	444	636	224

SOUTH MELVILLE	710	631	235
MELVILLE 3	226	451	184
MORTON	520	927	268
NORTH NEWLIN	343	457	144
SOUTH NEWLIN	163	260	81
PATTERSON	259	590	170
PLEASANT GROVE	766	302	90
NORTH THOMPSON	322	383	132
SOUTH THOMPSON	428	480	221
ABSENTEE	471	682	150
Total	15521	20637	6444

[Libertarian votes totaled 99 for the district]

11-3-1992 Results   Governor, Lt. Gov., Sec. Of State, State Auditor

A   James B.(Jim) Hunt   (D)
B   Jim Garner   (R)
C   Scott McLaughlin   (L)
D   Dennis A. Wicker   (D)
E   Art Pope   (R)
F   Jeanette C. Small   (L)
G   Rufus L. Edmisten   (D)
H   John H. Carrington   (R)
I   H.R. (Dick) Parker, Jr. (L)
J   Ralph Campbell   (D)
K   J. Vernon Abernethy   (D)
L   Harlan E. Boyles   (R)

(D)

	A	B	C	D	E	F	G	H	I	J	K	L
	For Gov			For Lieuten Gov			For Sec. Of State			For State Auditor		
ALBRIGHT CENTRAL	380	643	53	388	585	45	362	626	27	316	591	386

BOONE	558	729	69	465	780	49	448	827	41	389	833	506
NORTH BOONE	561	611	52	508	603	48	423	676	40	410	661	482
SOUTH BOONE	718	970	63	631	978	65	554	1055	54	520	1030	660
WEST BOONE	405	405	60	371	428	34	338	469	27	322	455	356
BOONE 5 EAST	502	717	57	459	698	47	460	709	46	439	691	477
BURLINGTON NORTH	381	504	48	386	479	42	381	487	33	369	488	414
BURLINGTON SOUTH	1321	373	37	1306	347	31	1296	388	23	1286	369	1299
BURLINGTON WEST	333	238	34	349	224	23	334	237	21	327	237	342
BURLINGTON 5	584	636	89	541	614	75	518	685	53	491	669	549
BURLINGTON 6	514	678	65	480	622	52	429	692	36	363	670	486
BURLINGTON 7	1039	1118	94	925	1083	65	835	1205	49	753	1154	877
BURLINGTON 8	1020	397	30	1013	358	27	999	375	22	990	372	1003
BURLINGTON 9	601	384	55	580	397	36	562	418	32	564	407	578
	598	800	80	582	774	59	532	856	36	523	827	630
COBLE	421	873	51	386	863	54	385	885	35	354	881	466
FAUCETTE	364	648	63	382	593	64	386	612	48	342	627	409

EAST GRAHAM	680	671	38	623	630	54	605	690	30	570	654	654
NORTH GRAHAM	585	455	47	580	427	39	554	457	36	573	428	598
SOUTH GRAHAM	990	1409	115	981	1333	97	917	1441	69	884	1415	1040
WEST GRAHAM	298	411	39	276	387	40	272	403	28	284	382	289
GRAHAM 3	733	791	46	711	763	42	691	780	34	697	764	742
HAW RIVER NORTH	965	599	48	946	578	41	929	598	32	904	580	977
MELVILLE SOUTH	631	669	38	630	598	28	559	666	22	538	627	611
MELVILLE	879	696	39	868	632	51	794	713	28	781	660	831
MELVILLE 3	365	480	66	368	457	37	330	505	31	300	490	356
MORTON	705	859	81	681	810	57	685	816	33	606	805	690
NORTH NEWLIN	422	466	40	426	408	34	385	451	31	369	424	397
SOUTH NEWLIN	202	281	24	199	268	25	195	281	22	184	283	212
PATTERSON	362	622	47	356	624	19	341	643	21	317	651	376
PLEASANT GROVE NORTH	862	340	27	860	296	19	861	286	22	826	284	860
THOMPSON SOUTH	440	360	32	405	342	27	378	378	28	360	361	411

THOMPSON		561	533	46	515	494	45	504	510	31	479	493	495
ABSENTEE		619	340	57	568	324	55	541	362	41	503	339	531
Total	20599	20,711	1830	19,745	19797	1526	18783	21182	1162	17933	20602	19990	

L

11/9/94   1994 GENERAL ELECTION
OFFICE DETAIL REPORT
FOR COUNTY COMMISSIONERS

a.   T. FRANK BENNETT - DEM
b.   R. HENDERSON SCOTT - DEM
c.   Timothy D. Sutton - Rep
d.   W.B. Junior Teague - Rep

Precinct	a.	b.	c.	d.
ALBRIGHT	175	226	468	509
CENTRAL BOONE	355	322	514	638
NORTH BOONE	291	272	439	467
SOUTH BOONE	334	315	634	715
WEST BOONE	194	187	294	332
BOONE 5	214	230	503	551
EAST BURLINGTON	155	165	296	319
NORTH BURLINGTON	678	701	232	254
SOUTH BURLINGTON	122	120	161	186
WEST BURLINGTON	338	343	404	467
BURLINGTON 4	328	280	373	434

BURLINGTON 5	253	262	475	526
BURLINGTON 6	335	287	450	522
BURLINGTON 7	458	457	271	283
BURLINGTON 8	263	256	218	246
BURLINGTON 9	253	269	543	600
COBLE	199	204	652	741
FAUCETTE	246	257	445	503
EAST GRAHAM	360	389	461	568
NORTH GRAHAM	235	260	329	362
SOUTH GRAHAM	247	283	463	505
WEST GRAHAM	128	116	269	307
GRAHAM 3	338	335	508	565
GRAHAM 4	299	304	585	667
HAW RIVER	410	462	397	448
NORTH MELVILLE	302	322	400	413
SOUTH MELVILLE	364	437	408	477
MELVILLE 3	178	256	321	383
MORTON	349	354	592	667
NORTH NEWLIN	194	264	318	372
SOUTH NEWLIN	90	112	181	219

PATTERSON	152	167	481	573
PLEASANT GROVE	492	520	234	252
NORTH THOMPSON	183	222	252	280
SOUTH THOMPSON	188	275	406	480
ABSENTEE	149	166	272	293
EDTV	1	4	7	8
TOTAL	9850	10401	14256	16132

Printed in the United States
46920LVS00002B/283